Manhood and Masculine Identity in William Shakespeare's *The Tragedy of Macbeth*

Maria L. Howell

UNIVERSITY PRESS OF AMERICA,® INC.
Lanham • Boulder • New York • Toronto • Plymouth, UK

Copyright © 2008 by
University Press of America,® Inc.
4501 Forbes Boulevard
Suite 200
Lanham, Maryland 20706
UPA Acquisitions Department (301) 459-3366

Estover Road
Plymouth PL6 7PY
United Kingdom

All rights reserved
Printed in the United States of America
British Library Cataloging in Publication Information Available

Library of Congress Control Number: 2008926475
ISBN-13: 978-0-7618-4074-9 (paperback : alk. paper)
ISBN-10: 0-7618-4074-5 (paperback : alk. paper)
eISBN-13: 978-0-7618-4198-2
eISBN-10: 0-7618-4198-9

∞™ The paper used in this publication meets the minimum
requirements of American National Standard for Information
Sciences—Permanence of Paper for Printed Library Materials,
ANSI Z39.48—1984

This book is dedicated to J.M.J., to my parents, Jack Williams (1907–1972), and Cecilia Williams—nee Warns (1914–1990), and to my family, especially, my daughter, Amanda, for their unfailing love, support and commitment. I would also like to acknowledge and pay tribute to Louis A. Montrose for his generosity and patience in reading and re-reading numerous drafts of my manuscript, and for inspiring me to achieve nothing less than the highest standards of academic excellence.

Contents

I	Introduction	1
II	Sexual Constructions of the Body	5
III	Gender and Power	11
IV	Concepts of Manhood and Masculine Identity	19
V	Elements of Tragedy	35
VI	Conclusion	40
Works Cited		43
Index		47

Chapter I
Introduction

Throughout William Shakespeare's works, the notion of "masculinity" and "masculine identity" is a recurrent thematic component. As a man living in a patriarchal society in Elizabethan England, Shakespeare was keenly cognizant of the anxieties endemic to masculine identity that he dramatizes. Shakespeare's history plays are a meditation on the ways masculine identity is constituted and defined by a man's relationship to his father, son or brother. The comedies provide an exploration of notions of manhood and masculine honor and how masculinity plays out between the sexes in courtship, marriage and parenthood. It is in the tragedies, however, that the extraordinary acts of greatness and feats of courage of the tragic hero are dramatized that "def[y] description, an excess, as it were, of virtue,"[1] that Shakespeare returns again and again to the question that Hamlet posed: "What is a man?"[2]

This work will focus on a textual analysis of Shakespeare's *Macbeth* in which I will analyze the concept of "manhood" dramatized throughout the play. I will make the argument that although *Macbeth* is not a repudiation of the cult of heroic masculinity, Shakespeare's scrutiny of the heroic ideal suggests that he did not accept these values without criticism. I will, therefore, argue that central to the understanding of the play is the question "What is a man?" How do we define his masculinity? What values constitute true manhood? I will argue that a dichotomy that constitutes masculine power and authority, paradoxically constrains and circumscribes man's autonomy and independence.

An examination of the notion of masculinity necessarily entails the examination of the dialectical relationship between genders. This analysis will, therefore, examine the complexity of the dialectical relationship between socially constructed notions of gender and sexuality within an Elizabethan cultural context and how this interplay reinforces and articulates relationships of power. Although Elizabethan cultural constructions of gender and sexuality are essentially autonomous entities, they are nonetheless interrelated, to each other and to relevant social, cultural and political practices of the sixteenth century.[3] *Macbeth* thus becomes a site of cultural production in which notions of manhood are not only articulated and addressed, but also contested and challenged.

The Oxford English Dictionary definition of the term "masculinity" in early modern English is essentially a biological concept, analogous to the term "maleness" or "manliness" in modern English (*OED 'masculine' 1.a*).[4] Bruce R. Smith in *Shakespeare and Masculinity* states that is only in the 1620s that the term "masculinity" came to signify attributes or characteristics associated with male behavior (*OED 'masculine' 5*).[5] However, Robin Headlam Wells in *Shakespeare on Masculinity* argues that while it is correct that most writers in the early modern period did not associate the term "masculinity" with behaviors deemed essentially masculine, the term "masculine" in Shakespeare's day signified martial qualities—physical strength, prowess in battle, and masculine honor—embodied in the heroic ideal.[6] Established in the Middle Ages, chivalry is a code of values that sanctioned and legitimized violence in defense of aristocratic notions of honor and justice. In the Renaissance, these values came into conflict with the humanistic understanding of man. Influenced by classical philosophers, humanists believed that man's reason was more intrinsic to his nature than "the use of the body."[7]

Fundamental to an understanding of masculine identity in the sixteenth century was the consolidation of power and authority in the male as both husband and father. According to Lawrence Stone, the increase of paternal sovereignty in the home was engendered by the convergence of two forces: the political and the religious.[8] In the political realm, traditional ties of the Crown to the feudal aristocracy, based on family lineage, were superseded by ties to the immediate family, thereby securing loyalty to the Crown in lieu of the feudal aristocracy. The State further consolidated patriarchy's near-absolute rule in the home by implementing the traditional analogy between the king, as head of the state, and the father, as head of the family.[9] The family was seen as a fundamental building block of society where deference to superiors and authorities was first learned and propagated. Obedience to paternal authority was analogous to obedience to the king. Second, with the rise of Protestantism, Puritan interpretations of scripture reinforced the role of the father as the head of the household, thus further consolidating paternal power in the home.[10]

In an attempt to analyze the concept of manhood in *Macbeth*, this work explores the contradictions and ambiguities that underlie heroic notions of masculinity dramatized throughout the play. In Chapter II, I will examine the constructed nature of sexual difference in the sixteenth century and how Lady Macbeth's desire to transcend her feminine nature reinforces and exacerbates patriarchal anxieties of female sexuality during the early modern period. In Chapter III, I will examine the dialectical relationship between genders dramatized throughout the play and how Lady Macbeth's capacity to control and destroy Macbeth's masculine identity reinforces patriarchal fears of feminine desire in early modern England. In Chapter IV of this study, I will examine how heroic notions of masculinity not only reinforce masculine power and authority, but paradoxically are the source of man's disempowerment and destruction. Thus, I will examine in this section how heroic values, if given legitimacy, become the greatest threat to society and to man himself, reinforcing one of the most polemic issues in the sixteenth century: the deposition of tyrants. In Chapter V, I will explore how Shakespeare shapes the play into a tragedy and discuss the ramifications of Macbeth's defiance and lack of repentance, which prevents the play from achieving full closure

NOTES

1. Torquato Tasso, *Della Virtu Eroica e Della Carita* qtd. in Robin Headlam Wells, *Shakespeare on Masculinity* (Cambridge: University Press 2000) 2.

2. William Shakespeare, *Tragedy of Hamlet,* ed. Sylvan Barnet, 2nd ed. (New York: Penguin, 1998) 4.4 33.

3. Gayle Rubin, "The Traffic in Women: Notes toward a 'Political Economy' of Sex" in *Toward an Anthropology of Women,* ed. Rayna R. Rieter (New York: Monthly Review P, 1975) 157–210.

4. In the Introduction to his work *Shakespeare and Masculinity*, Bruce R. Smith cites the work of anthropologist, David Gilmore, who explores the notion of masculinity through historical and cultural dimensions. Smith states that Gilmore's work reveals that "masculinity is something quite different from biological maleness" and that masculinity comes to mean different things in different cultures. According to Smith, the one constant variable determined by Gilmore is that masculinity is not axiomatic but rather is *achieved* (Smith 2). See Bruce R. Smith, *Shakespeare and Masculinity* (Oxford: Oxford University Press, 2000) 2.

5. Smith 11.

6. Robin Headlam Wells, *Shakespeare on Masculinity* (Cambridge: University Press 2000) 21.

7. Aristotle argues in *The Art of Rhetoric* that in the area of self-defense, rhetoric is an important instrument "since reason is a more particular human property than the

use of the body." See Aristotle, *The Art of Rhetoric* trans. H.C. Lawson-Trancred (London: Penguin, 1991), 69.

8. Coppelia Kahn, *Man's Estate: Masculine Identity in Shakespeare* (London: University of California Press, 1981), 12–13.

9. Kahn 13.

10. Khan 13.

Chapter II

Sexual Constructions of the Body

Well before Shakespeare's time, the inferiority of women was assumed *a priori* simply by virtue of their creation from the rib of Adam. During the early modern period, however, the inferiority of the female was further inscribed with notions which had ideological and political ramifications. Galenic theories of the body in the sixteenth century held that the body was a function of the four humors—blood, phlegm, yellow, and black bile—and the corresponding four elements.[1] For the most part, therefore, male and female bodies were anatomically homologous and there was little or no difference between them. Men's ability to produce "heat" caused their sexual organs to protrude outwards. Women's *inability* to produce "heat" and their predisposition toward cold and moist humors, caused their sexual organs to invert inwards. The female uterus and womb were thus an inverted phallus. Galenic theories of body thus constituted the female as an inferior version of the male. The formulation of gender and sexual notions of the body in the sixteenth century therefore reinforced the superiority of the male and consolidated patriarchy's near-absolute authority over the female.

I submit that a patriarchal system designed to reinforce masculine power and authority paradoxically constitutes the female as its locus of vulnerability in that any passionate relationship will endanger or threaten his masculine identity. That is, the extreme polarization of social roles and behavior that constitutes the masculine as strong, fearless and resolute, devoid of feeling and tenderness, essentially become compromised in his relationship with the female. This liaison would, in effect, contaminate his masculine virtue, rendering him weak and effeminate, resulting ultimately in the loss of his manhood.

As is evidenced by his letter to Lady Macbeth, this becomes a reality in Macbeth's life. Written after his great military victory, his expression of profound love—"my dearest partner of greatness"—is a manifestation not only of his deep admiration and affection, but also of his feelings of trust, loyalty, and esteem. Lady Macbeth is more than his wife—she is his love, his confidant, his ally, closely linked with him in his ambitious cause. Unquestionably, they are like-minded in their quest for power. At first glance, it appears that their marriage is indeed a partnership of co-equals. On closer inspection, however, a different reality begins to emerge. First and foremost, the letter contains a circular feeling of trepidation. In the beginning of the letter, Macbeth feels compelled to authenticate the veracity of the witches' prediction that he will be king as a way to preserve his own masculine integrity and to prove that the predictions are not a figment of his imagination. He concludes by stating that the reason for his writing was to inform and assure her of "what greatness is promised *Thee*" so that she will waste no time in "rejoicing" (1.5. 11). While his overt gesture of deference is meant to reaffirm his love and affection, Macbeth's uncanny choice of words "what greatness is promised *Thee*" conceals a different reality—that perhaps masculine power is invested not in himself, but rather in Lady Macbeth.

This becomes particularly evident in Lady Macbeth's response to his letter. Unlike Macbeth, who sees the predictions as a "promise of greatness," an event that could or might happen in the future, Lady Macbeth's reaction is more certain, absolute, and unequivocal, "Glamis thou art, and Cawdor; and shalt be/ What thou art promised" (1.4. 13–14). Lady Macbeth's self-assurance and resolute purpose, characteristics associated with the masculine, affirm her power and authority and, by implication, confirm Macbeth's lack. Her response, moreover, echoes the predictions of the witches, reinforcing the notion that like the witches, Lady Macbeth is a destabilizing force that threatens to undo Macbeth. Lady Macbeth's indubitable belief that Macbeth will be king is again manifested in her greeting when Macbeth returns home. Unlike Macbeth's expression of affection "my dearest love," Lady Macbeth's triple greetings, "Great Glamis / Worth Cawdor / Greater than both by the all-hail hereafter" (1.5. 16–17), not only resonates with the witches' predictions at the beginning of the play, it leaves no doubt that Lady Macbeth sees the kingship as a reality which has already come into being. The image that his letter has "transported [her] beyond / This ignorant present, and I feel now / The future in the instant" (1.5. 55–57), evokes a collapsed metaphysical reality in which all time has been erased. Lady Macbeth no longer lives in the present but rather sees the kingship as a reality, something that is concrete, tangible, not only within Macbeth's grasp, but already vested in him and which inheres in him as king. Unlike the witches who merely seduce and entice Macbeth with the promise of grandeur and majesty, Lady Macbeth is a dangerous and lethal force. As his wife, she becomes that threatening force that imperils Macbeth's masculine virtue that will ultimately result in the loss of his manhood.

Shakespeare thus exposes an underlying anxiety endemic to masculine identity in early modern England. I will make the argument that if "heat" is the only factor that differentiates man from woman, then given the fungible nature of humors, any passionate desire for a woman may, in all probability, endanger his masculinity, turning a man into a woman.[2] Stephen Orgel argues: "The frightening part of the teleology for the Renaissance mind . . . [is] precisely the fantasy of its reversal, the conviction that men can turn into—or be turned into—women; or perhaps more exactly, can be turned back into women, losing the strength that enabled the male potential to be realized in the first place."[3] Janet Adelman also argues that "a merger with a female would mean the end of his hard won masculine selfhood."[4]

In dramatizing the reversion of gender roles, Shakespeare exposes the performative nature of masculinity in early modern England. Manhood was not seen as axiomatic but rather acquired and asserted through performance. Bruce R. Smith argues: "Masculinity is a matter of contingency, of circumstances, of performance."[5] It is Macbeth's unadulterated masculine virtue as "Valor's minion" (1.2. 21) that attests to his quintessential masculinity.[6] By "unseam[ing]" Macdonwald from the "nave to the chops," Macbeth destroys the rebel Macdonwald, whose dalliance with *Fortune*, "the rebel's whore" (1.2. 17), weakens and corrupts his sense of manliness. Moreover, Ross' play on the word "double" in "As canons overcharged with *double* cracks, / so they *doubly redoubled* strokes upon the foe" (1.2. 37–38), underscores Macbeth's unrelenting prowess and indubitable ferocity. Duncan's exaltation of Macbeth's military skills: "O, valiant cousin! Worthy gentleman" (1.2. 24), illustrates that heroic masculinity acquires its mythical status by and through the praises of men. This notion is reinforced by Bruce Smith who states that "masculine identity of whatever kind is something men give to each other. It is not achieved in isolation."[7]

In dramatizing these contradictions, Shakespeare exposes the constructed nature of gender polarities as arbitrary, unstable, and elusive. They are not mutually exclusive, but rather one category exists at the expense of the other. In conceding dominance to men, patriarchy's gender prescriptions essentially categorize woman as the gendered "other" whose subordination is not only necessary, but essential to the continuation of man's identity. Smith argues that "If 'man' needs 'woman' in order to be 'man', then womanliness will constantly be threatened to erupt from within."[8]

While the play confirms and legitimizes hierarchical notions of patriarchal power and authority, it simultaneously questions and subverts those structures. In Act 1, Scene 5, for example, Lady Macbeth's desire to transcend her female nature and thus become the embodiment of the heroic ideal, subverts a system that seeks to subordinate her. Lady Macbeth sees her female nature—compassion, sympathy, kindness, and love—as detrimental and hazardous to her perceived purposes. Thus, she must be made impervious to (and shielded from) her conscience and from guilt. This necessitates that she suppress the workings of nature so that she will no longer experience menstruation, a function that binds her to childbirth, creation, and nature itself, "make thick my blood / Stop up th'access and passage to remorse, / That no compunctious visitings of nature / Shake my fell purpose, / Come to my woman's breasts, / And take my milk for gall (1.5. 42–47). The play thus evokes Aristotelian notions of the body, prevalent during the sixteenth century, in which the inseminating power of the male was seen as superior to the "corrupted" seed of the female and, therefore, incapable of generation. "The seede . . . is white in man by reason of his greate heate, and because it is digested better . . . The seede of a woman is red . . . because the flower is corrupt, undigested blood" (Problems of Aristotle, sig. E3r).[9] The female body is thus a mere "vessel," a giver of material substance that sustains and nurtures life, and therefore not a propagator of life. The phallocentric power of the male is seen as the procreator of both life and spirit that provides not only the soul, but human life. Aristotelian theories of the body further reinforced the inferiority of the female by promulgating that mortality was inherited from the "deformed female body." The womb thus becomes, "a malevolent power quite divorced from the largely powerless women who might be supposed to embody it."[10] The play therefore articulates a hierarchical notion of gender relations in which the male body becomes a site of power, through and upon which power is socially constructed, mediated, and legitimated. That is, the male body in the sixteenth century is socially constructed as the source of all power, because it is from man that all life flows. In contrast, the female body is associated with the material and the corruptible forces of nature.

I submit that by denying women their feminine nature in order to reinforce paternal power and authority, patriarchy paradoxically constitutes the female body as that inscrutable force of nature that threatens, challenges, and undermines its power. By invoking demonic forces to "unsex" her, and "fill [her] from top to toe with direst cruelty," (1.5. 42–44), Lady Macbeth becomes, in the beginning of the play, the embodiment of that enigmatic feminine force who, like the witches, is a source of chaos, violence and instability, which threatens to disrupt and undo masculine power and authority. Like the witches, whose genders are also nebulous, contradictory, and ambiguous, Lady Macbeth becomes the embodiment of what Cristina Alfar defines as the "female evil," shaped out of patriarchy's anxieties about the female body and their inability to control it.[11]

In dramatizing these events, Shakespeare exposes an underlying fear endemic to patriarchy in the sixteenth century. Elizabeth A. Foyster argues that in the early modern period, the "key to male power in the household was thought to be sexual control of women as well as the self."[12] Her analysis gives us an interesting light into the underlying anxieties engendered by female sexuality during this period. Since fatherhood validated a man's identity, I will argue that it is precisely because women's sexuality remained an enigma, incomprehensible, and unknowable, and therefore uncontrollable and uncontainable, that patriarchal fears were exacerbated and reinforced.[13] Since marriage in the early modern period was a means to establishing not only rightful heirs to name and property, but also economic relations between men, chastity became not only a moral imperative, but an economic one as well. Breitenberg argues that "in early modern England, the masculine discourse demanding sexual chastity in women is always additionally shaped by an anxiety about the preservation or pollution of an ideal of class purity. Or, in other terms, a status system dependent on the 'proper' dissemination of property and title between men literally and symbolically requires the assurance of female chastity and virginity."[14]

Cristina Alfar argues that the notion of "feminine evil" thus becomes an explicit discourse of conduct manuals during the early modern period.[15] Vives saw infidelity and loss of chastity as analogous to treason, since the husband, as head of his wife, is synonymous to the king as the head of his subjects.[16] Moreover, the extraordinary number of plays in the sixteenth and seventeenth centuries which dramatized "cuckoldry" attests to the immediacy of this issue and the growing anxiety endemic to masculine identity.

In this Chapter, I have demonstrated that to the extent that masculine power and authority is contingent on the chastity of women, this power, to a large extent, is tenuous, arbitrary and unstable. As the play illustrates, female sexuality remained a conundrum that was unknowable, uncontrollable, and always in contest. Absent any clear evidence to the contrary, men could never be certain that their wives would remain faithful to them. It was man's inability to control female chastity that inevitably gave rise to men's fears and anxieties. Thus, patriarchy's prescriptions of gender in the early modern not only constituted masculine power and authority, they paradoxically exacerbated and undermined it.

NOTES

1. Smith 4.
2. In explicating the nature of melancholy, Mark Breitenberg in *Anxious Maculinity in Early Modern Englan*d explores the humoural effects on the body. Following on from Gail Kern Paster's humoural psychology, he argues that the individual "assumes an essential sameness among the materials that make up the psyche" which is "the result of degrees and propensities of the same materials, or humours." This is due, he

explains, to the fact that "the fluids that comprise the body are fungible; that is, they are transformed from one to another, as in the belief that semen derives from blood." He goes on to states that "This means that in theory everyone has the potential to possess or enact the entire spectrum of human characteristics and desires that derive from the balance (or imbalance) of fluids in the body" (38). *See* Mark Mark Breitenberg, *Anxious Maculinity in Early Modern England*, Cambridge Studies in Renaissance Literature and Culture (Cambridge: UP, 1996), 38.

3. Stephen Orgel, "Nobody's Perfect: Or, Why Did the English Stage Take Boys for Women?" qtd. in Breitenberg 14.

4. Janet Adelman, *Suffocating Mothers: Fantasies of Maternal Origin in Shakespeare's Plays*, Hamlet *to* The Tempest (New York: Routledge, 1992).

5. Smith 60.

6. In the Renaissance, a new and important concept that influenced and defined the notion of manhood was the relationship between *virtu* and *fortune*. Derived partly from Italian realpolitik, v*irtu* was seen to exist within the individual. It was defined by a certain astuteness and reflected man's capacity to master circumstances and to turn to his advantage those opportunities which might otherwise be beyond his capacity to attain. *Fortune* was seen to exist external to man, whereby events occurred through chance, luck and happenstance. It was man's capacity to gain dominance over *fortune* that allowed him then to master and control events. See Felix Gilbert, *Fortune, Necessity, Virtu* in Niccolo Machiavelli, *The Prince*, trans. and ed. Robert M. Adams, 2nd ed. (New York: Norton 1992) 150–55.

7. Smith 14.

8. Smith 14.

9. *The Problemes of Aristotle, with other Philosophers and Phisitions* (London: Arnold Hatfield, 1597) sigs E3-E4; qtd. in Louis Montrose, "Shaping Fantasies: Figurations of Gender and Power in Elizabethan Culture, *Representing the English Renaissance*, ed. Stephen Greenblatt (Berkeley: U of California P,1988), 43. Montrose argues that this text conflates Galenic and Aristotelian theories of procreation.

10. Adelman 9.

11. Cristina Leon Alfar, *Fantasies of Female Evil: The Dynamics of Gender and Power in Shakespearean Tragedy* (Newark: U of Delaware P, 2003), 31.

12. Foyster 4.

13. Alfar 31. The following quote by Julia Kristeva was cited by Alfar. Kristeva argues "woman's mutability, the challenge to dominion and restraint that the indeterminacy of her body's secretions, rhythms, and expulsions is exacerbated by the failure of the masculinist order to contain her fluidity, her inconstancy, rendering her a demonized threat."

14. Breitenberg 70.

15. Alfar 31. Alfar expounds further in this chapter on conduct manuals and their attempt to placate masculine anxieties over the female body.

16. Alfar 39.

Chapter III

Gender and Power

The body was not only signifier of sexual disparity in the sixteenth century, it served as an analogy for gender difference in which the subordinated status of the female was a manifestation of her social and political inequality. In this chapter I will explore the dynamics of gender and power dramatized throughout the play in which Lady Macbeth undermines culturally sanctioned norms of masculine identity. I will make the argument that in predicating masculine identity on the suppression of female desire, patriarchy paradoxically constitutes the female as that frightening figure that threatens and challenges men's power and authority.

In Act 1, Scene 5, for example, Lady Macbeth's desire to persuade Macbeth to murder the king: "Hie thee thither, / that I may pour my spirits in thine ear, / And chastise with the valor of my tongue" (24–26), envisions a world of relentless persuasion, indefatigable resolution and resolute purpose. She sees herself not only as a catalyst for change, but also as the source of masculine power, which will transform Macbeth into the epitome of the heroic ideal. Rather than being the moral compass, leading her husband back from his errant ways, Lady Macbeth becomes instead the instrument of his corruption.

By subverting her conventional feminine role, Lady Macbeth's actions legitimize structures of patriarchal power and authority while affirming the subordinated status of the female. Puritan minister and writer in the sixteenth century, William Gouge, defended the subordination of wives to their husbands, echoing sentiments reiterated in the Homily of Marriage preached throughout the year: "wives submit yourselves unto your divine husbands, as unto the Lord . . . for the husband is the head of the wife, even as Christ is the head of the Church."[1] Lady Macbeth's actions thus constitute a transgression of her societal gender role.

By persuading Macbeth to murder the king, Lady Macbeth becomes the embodiment of patriarchal fears of feminine desire that threatens the masculine imperative of will and action, and thus his power and authority. Like Eve, Lady Macbeth incites men to evil by breaking laws essential to the stability of society. Her actions thus constitute a fundamental act of betrayal and treason, to suggest that women are a dangerous threat to the social order and thus to the stability of the realm. Her actions, moreover, lend credence to the belief held in the Renaissance that "Evil persuasion, especially of the kind which encourages fundamental betrayal, is a natural attribute of the Machiavelle."[2]

According to Alfar, it is precisely by virtue of their gender, and thus their affiliation with Eve, that women in the early modern period were denied access to power and thus denied the ability to participate in the creation of civic laws. She states, "the relationship between civil and religious law is apparent in *The Law's Resolutions of Women's Rights*, which argues for women's subjection to men, and therefore to laws, based on their sisterhood with Eve: 'Eve because she had helped to seduce her husband hath inflicted on her an especial bane . . . See here the reason of that which I touched before, that women have no voice in parliament. They make no laws, they consent to none, they abrogate none . . . The common law here shaketh hand with divinity.'"[3] The inferiority of women therefore had greater ideological and political ramifications in early modern England.

By inciting Macbeth to evil, Lady Macbeth's actions expose an underlying contradiction inherent in patriarchy in early modern England. Disempowered in the realm of the political, women become duplicitous and dangerous, seeking to achieve covertly what has been denied to them overtly. In Act 1, Scene 5, for example, Lady Macbeth counsels her husband to appear natural and innocent as a "flower" enabling him, like the "serpent under't," to conduct his evil deeds in secret: "To beguile the time, / Look like the time; bear welcome in your eye. / Your hand, your tongue; look like the innocent flower, / But be the serpent under't. (1.5. 63–66).[4] The "serpent" evokes an image of evil and clearly connects Lady Macbeth to the demonic forces of darkness. The image resonates with the Biblical figure of Eve in the Garden of Eden, whose seduction of Adam leads to the fall of mankind from God's grace, to suggest that Lady Macbeth, like Eve, will become the instrument of Macbeth's downfall, leading ultimately to his destruction and death. The serpent, therefore, becomes synonymous with the feminine: cunning, dangerous, and deceitful.

This is particularly evident in Act 1, Scene 6, when Duncan arrives at Macbeth's castle. Like the "sightless" forces of evil, Lady Macbeth is the epitome of grace and hospitality, assuring the king of their devotion and service. At the same time her gesture of deference and solicitude conceals her treacherous plan to murder Duncan, an act which constitutes a fundamental betrayal of the bonds of loyalty, friendship, and hospitality. Her admission that any service and hospitality they render him, even if "twice done and then done double" (1.6. 15) is nothing compared to the honors he has bestowed on them, echoes the discourse of the witches, "Double, double, toil and trouble" (4.1. 20), to suggest that like the witches, Lady Macbeth is a destabilizing force who has the power to disrupt the governance of the realm. In predicating masculine identity on the suppression of female desire, patriarchy thus provides women with an avenue of resistance.

Lady Macbeth's rhetorical act of persuasion thus give voice to one of the greatest political, social and cultural issues in the Renaissance—the cultivation of rhetoric as an art of persuasion. According to A. McAlindon, to humanists in the sixteenth century, the "tongue came to be seen the as the greatest instrument of good, as well as evil."[5] Humanists believed that language had the power persuade, to appeal to man's imagination, to inspire him to envision a greater moral reality which would then move him to action. In the opening chapter of *The Art of Rhetoric,* Aristotle argues that "rhetoric is the counterpart of dialectic" in which all men from all walks of life engage and participate, whether in law or politics."[6] Thus, the notion of communicating, of inspiring man to action through eloquence and language was the central proposition of rhetoric, reaffirming the Renaissance notion of action over contemplation. Aristotle argues, moreover, that in the area of self-defense, rhetoric is an important instrument, "since reason is a more particular human property than the use of the body."[7] Thus, Macduff's sword, "I have no words: / My voice is my sword" (5.7. 43–44), is metaphorically transformed in the Renaissance to the "voice of persuasion." Diplomacy and rational discourse now achieve in peace and equanimity, that which the sword secured in battle and military conflict.

Moreover, with the discovery of classical texts and in line with humanist philology in the sixteenth century, rhetoric gained prominence as a didactic tool to instill moral values. In Renaissance mythography, Ovid's Orpheus was celebrated as the "founder of civilization" for his ability to tame the wildest inhabitants of the Underworld. Through the power of eloquence and music, Orpheus begged for the return of his wife, until the "the pale phantoms were in tears: Ixion's wheel /Was still, Tityos' vultures left the liver, /Tantalus tried no more to reach for the water, / And Belus' daughters rested from their urns, /And Sisyphus climbed on his rock to listen. /That was the first time ever in all the world / The Furies wept." (Book X. 24–31).[8] J. C. Scaliger argues that "the soul of persuasion is truth, truth either fixed and absolute, or susceptible of question. Its end is to convince, or to secure the doing of something '"[9] St. Augustine in *The Confessions* claims that it was the eloquence of Saint Ambrose that set him on the right path, that ended ultimately in his full conversion to Christianity.

Lady Macbeth not only persuades Macbeth to evil, she endeavors to destroy Macbeth's faith in himself. For example, in impugning Macbeth's masculinity when he reneges on his promise to kill Duncan, "When you durst do it, then you were a man; / And, to be more than what you were, you would / Be so much more the man" (1.7. 49–51), Lady Macbeth reinforces masculine notions of ambition and desire, and at the same undermines and negates Macbeth's volition and power to act. In addition, the imagery of impotence and powerlessness evoked by Lady Macbeth "Was the hope drunk / Wherein you dressed yourself? Hath it slept since?/ And wakes it now, to look so green and pale / At what it did so freely"(1.7. 39–42), suggests that Macbeth only has the courage to act when he is under the influence of alcohol and that on becoming sober, he loses his nerve and becomes "pale and green." The imagery of phallic impotency resonates with sentiments evoked by the porter in Act 3, Scene 2, in which he claims that like lechery, alcohol, "provokes the desire, but it takes away the performance . . . it makes him, and it mars, it sets him on, and takes him off" (3.2. 25–28), to suggest that Macbeth's masculine virtue is not innate, but rather is induced by a substance external to him. Lady Macbeth further denigrates Macbeth's masculinity by implying that, like a drunkard, Macbeth has lost the use of his reason and become irrational and chaotic, characteristics associated with the feminine.[10] Her evocation of bestial imagery, "What beast was't then / That made you break this enterprise to me?" (1.7. 53–54) is therefore not without cultural resonance. Foyster argues: "Moralists warned that men who were drunk lost their reason could slip into a bestial state, becoming little different from the brutish Swine."[11]

Lady Macbeth's attack on Macbeth's reason is, in effect, an attack on his manhood. Beginning with Plato, Western thought held that reason was the predominant attribute of the male, a characteristic that distinguished man from the female. Foyster argues that in the early modern period, reason constituted and legitimated male authority over women. Drunkenness and its implied loss of reason therefore had grave social and moral consequences. The loss of reason meant the loss of manhood. In essentially reducing Macbeth to a primitive animal, given to uncontrolled passions and a degraded sense of reason, Lady Macbeth's actions give voice to the discrepancy between patriarchy's power to subordinate women, and a woman's ability to usurp that power; between patriarchy's domination and control of women, and man's vulnerability to the power of women.[12]

This is particularly manifested in Lady Macbeth's chilling gesture that she will take her fragile and vulnerable new-born child who is feeding at her breast "and dash [its] brains out," (1, 7 64). Like Medea, Lady Macbeth's defiant gesture exposes the constructed nature of gender polarities that force women to kill their children to prove that they are not without resolve or purpose. Moreover, in a society in which patriarchal power and authority is secured from one generation to another through the male line, Lady Macbeth's desire to destroy her child, would essentially destroy Macbeth's ability to secure his power and authority through future generations. Lady Macbeth thus becomes the embodiment of patriarchy's anxieties of female desire and their ability to destroy the future.

Intimated by Lady Macbeth's act of defiance, Macbeth's exclamation, "Bring forth men-children only" (1.7. 81) reaffirms his admiration for her sense of masculine virtue and, by implication, confirms his lack. He suggests that given Lady Macbeth's inability to nurture and protect her young child, she is the perfect vessel to bring forth a future breed of killers. He thus evokes an image of Lady Macbeth as fulfilling both the maternal and paternal role: she is not merely an empty *vessel*, a *container,* but the giver of life and spirit as well. Perhaps it is not without accident that having been denied the ability to have an heir and thus the ability to create a dynasty, Macbeth, like Lady Macbeth, becomes an infanticide who murders and kills children in order to control the future. His actions lend credence to the intimation that despite his desire to achieve autonomy and independence from Lady Macbeth, he is indeed a creature of her design and a conduit of her dark and destructive spirit. Lady Macbeth thus becomes the frightening figure of feminine desire who, like Eve, incites man to evil by breaking *natural laws* fundamental to man's existence.

Unlike Lady Macbeth's desire to be a man which is seen as a transcendence of feminine and fragile nature, Macbeth's subordination to Lady Macbeth is seen as a degradation, the feminization of his masculine virtue which leads ultimately to the loss of his manhood. His capitulation to Lady Macbeth's desire to murder the king, "If we should fail?" (1.7. 66), reveals a man undone, completely "unmanned," reduced to a helpless child at the mercy of an all-consuming and all compassing maternal presence. Macbeth's repetition of the words, "I'll go no more," "I am afraid" and "I dare not" (2,3. 54–56), as he refuses to return the bloodied daggers to the murder scene, defies the heroic imperative of will and action and reinforces the notion that he has been emasculated and reduced to the role of the feminine. His sense of impotence and powerlessness suggest that in murdering Duncan, Macbeth has destabilized the normal functioning of his being so that his sense of internal coherence and well-being is disrupted and destroyed. He is distracted, disturbed, and destabilized and "every noise appalls [him]" (2.2. 74). The recognition that he could not say *Amen* in response to the servant's prayers, "But wherefore could not I say 'Amen'?/ I had most need of a blessing, 'Amen' / Stuck in my throat," (2.2. 41–43), suggests Macbeth has been deprived of, closed off from, shut out of his own spiritual essence and being, so that he can no longer comprehend the reality of his life. This notion is reinforced by his lament: "To know my deed, 'twere best not know myself" (2,2 73). Macbeth's sense of infantilization foreshadows similar sentiments of powerlessness and impotency in Act 3, Scene 4, when he learns that Fleance has escaped.

In contrast, Lady Macbeth, at this point in the play, is resolute and unwavering. Despite her inability to kill Duncan, she is indifferent and unaffected by his death and the murder of his servants, who she says "Are but as pictures" of themselves, devoid of life, soul, and identity, and thus have no essence (2.2. 69). With hands covered in blood, she returns the daggers to the murder scene, and chastises Macbeth for being a coward, "My hands are of your color, but I shame / To wear a heart so white" (2.2. 64–65). In assuming the role of the maternal, she reduces Macbeth to a whimpering child, ordering him to "Get on your nightgown" (2.2. 85), and attempting to assuage his guilt by suggesting "A little water clears us of this deed" (2.2. 83).

In dramatizing the reversal of gender roles, Shakespeare breaks the distinction between the feminine and the masculine and opens up an indeterminate space where gender identity is ambiguous and contradictory. In becoming subordinate to Lady Macbeth, Macbeth has in effect negated crucial differences between men and women and compromised the masculine imperative of reason, volition, and self-control. His behavior is antithetical to notions of heroic masculinity and threatens to endanger the very fabric of masculine power and authority. Breitenberg states that "the "manly woman" challenges a masculine economy of knowledge and interpretation by confusing the very act of interpretation a distinctively masculine prerogative in this patriarchal culture"[13] In becoming subordinate to Lady Macbeth, Macbeth becomes the "interpreted object," rather than the "interpreting subject," thus lending credence to the notion that gender in the early modern is a construct, constituted as a function of performance and interpretation.

However, according to Holinshed's historical narrative, from which Shakespeare drew his material, Lady Macbeth merely had an "unquenchable desire to be queen."[14] In ascribing to Lady Macbeth the attributes of Donwald's wife for dramatic purposes, who, according to Holinshed, "encouraged her husband to murder and showed him the means," Shakespeare created a more complex and contradictory character.[15] This permitted Shakespeare to give voice to an underlying fear endemic to masculine identity in the early modern period. According to Coppelia Kahn, patriarchal power belongs not so much to men in general as to the father acting as the head of a family."[16] I submit that since fatherhood validates a man's identity, it is precisely the fear of a woman's ability to control and destroy his masculine identity, thereby diminishing the gender difference men and women that exacerbates and reinforces masculine anxieties in early modern England. Given that an imbalance in humors could turn a man into a woman, or, as Orgel states, "can be turned back into women," *woman*, herself, becomes the enemy that threatens to destroy and disrupt masculine power and authority. Breitenberg argues that it is the fear of "sameness between men and women, a sameness always understood as regression or debasement on the part of men" that contributes to male anxieties in the sixteenth century.[17] It is the fear that men can "degenerate into women, to take the place of women"[18]

In this Chapter, I have illustrated that to the extent that masculine power and authority is contingent on the subordination of women and the suppression of female desire, this power, in the beginning of the play, is not assured and rarely achieved. As a result, men are constantly compelled to assert their masculinity in order to differentiate themselves from women, reinforcing the notion that the anatomical difference between genders is not guaranteed.[19] Shakespeare thus problematizes patriarchal norms of gender prescription to suggest that anxieties endemic to masculine identity in the early modern period have their source in patriarchal ideology itself. In the play, however, Shakespeare restores patriarchal norms of gender and power by dramatizing Lady Macbeth's complete alienation from the major action of the play and a return to her feminine role.

NOTES

1. Elizabeth A. Foyster, Manhood in Early Modern England: Honor Sex and Marriage (London: Longman, 1999).

2. T. McAlindon, English Renaissance Tragedy (Vancouver: U of British Columbia Press, 1986), 32.

3. Alfar 9.

4. Machiavelli advocated that rulers should convey the pretense of virtue in order to conceal their ambitious desires. See Niccolo Machiavelli, *The Prince*, trans. and ed. by Robert M. Adams, 2nd ed. (New York: Norton 1992), 47–49.

5. T. McAlindon 32.

6. Aristotle, The Art of Rhetoric, trans. H.C. Lawson-Tancred (London: Penguin Books, 1991), 66.

7. Aristotle 69.

8. Ovid, Metamorphoses, trans. Rolfe Humphries (Indianapolis: Indiana University Press, 1983) 235.

9. J. C. Scaliger qtd. in "Rhetoric and poetics," The Cambridge History of Renaissance Philosophy, eds. Quentin Skinner and Eckhard Kessler (New York: Cambridge University Press, 1988) 736.

10. Lacan theorizes that all subjectivity, identity and culture is constituted in terms of the "phallic." The "phallic" therefore is the signifier which constitutes man's

superiority and dominance over women, and reifies that dominance as natural. Women, by virtue of their lack of a phallus, constitute their difference as "lack" or "absence" (60). In further explicating Elizabeth Grosz' analysis of Lacanian conception of male and female subjectivities, Christina Alfar argues that the "phallus," therefore,"becomes the symbolic site of difference between men and women, that which distinguishes them from one another in culture and 'brings them together' in a union predicated on the fulfillment of masculine desire." (115) See Jacques Lacan, *The Meaning of the Phallus*, in Feminine Sexuality: Jacques Lacan and the Ecole Freudienne, trans. Jacqueline Rose, ed. Juliet Mitchell and Jacqueline Rose (New York: Norton, 1982), 60–80.

11. Foyster 6.

12. Unlike Lacan, Michel Foucault argues that gender is a system of classification which is culturally produced. How we interpret and understand these differences is constituted and reproduced through discourse. Discourse therefore assigns systems of meaning and becomes the framework whereby individuals understand and interpret the world. Foucault argues, however, that discourse is not the reflection of reality, but rather it is that with which reality becomes constituted. In seeking to transcend her feminine nature, Lady Macbeth participates in a discourse in which power and authority is vested in the masculine, and the feminine is constituted as weak, fragile and compliant and, therefore, devoid of power. Foucault argues, moreover, that wherever power is exercised, a resistant discourse emerges, thus empowering those who have been marginalized. He states: "Discourse transmits and produces power; it reinforces it; but also undermines and exposes it; renders it fragile and makes it possible to thwart it" (1476–1481). Thus, discourse has a multiplicity of meanings which vary according to the context. Discourse can thus be employed in reverse ways in diverse situations. See Michel Foucault, The History of Sexuality in *The Critical Tradition*, 2nd edition, ed. David H. Richter (Boston: Bedford 1998), (1472–1481).

13. Breitenberg 160.

14. Raphael Holinshed, *Selections from Chronicles of England, Scotland, and Ireland* in The Tragedy of Macbeth, ed. Sylvan Barnet. 2nd ed. (London: Penguin, 1998), 104.

15. Raphael Holinshed 111.

16. Kahn 12.

17. Breitenberg 162.

18. Breitenberg 162.

19. Mark Breitenberg argues "that from the perspective of anatomical science, we may thus understand masculine anxiety as a social phenomenon (arising from contradictions endemic to patriarchy) that is played out reciprocally in the male body, a body that is the site of socially constructed anxieties about sex and gender but is by no means their origin" (Breitenberg 14).

Chapter IV

Concepts of Manhood and Masculine Identity

In dramatizing Lady Macbeth's ability to subvert Macbeth's masculine identity, the play thus becomes a site of cultural production in which notions of manhood are not only validated and affirmed, but also interrogated and challenged. I will make the argument that a patriarchal system designed to validate man's power and authority, paradoxically undermines man's autonomy and independence of thought and action.

Despite his innate desire to be king, Macbeth, for example, knows that in committing regicide, he would be going against the moral order of the universe and that all of heaven would revolt. He knows, too, that in murdering the king, he would be setting a precedent and that he in turn may suffer the same fate. He knows that in killing Duncan who is his "kin," his "guest," and his king, he will be breaking laws of hospitality, loyalty, and solidarity, fundamental to the stability of society. Yet, compelled to authenticate his masculine virtue, Macbeth capitulates to Lady Macbeth's desires. Through this one act, his life changes irrevocably and forever.

In dramatizing Macbeth's rejection of communal bonds, Shakespeare underscores the importance of male friendships. Masculinity is not only achieved through the female/male relationship, it is also constituted and asserted through male friendships. According to Bruce Smith, friendship is an important component to understanding manhood in the early modern period. He states: "For Aristotle, and for his successors, Cicero, Montaigne, and Bacon, friendship between men who are social equals constitutes the most important human bond there is."[1] Friendship thus becomes an avenue through which manhood was achieved and affirmed. Smith argues, moreover, that "friendship also seems to be the bond that holds communities together, and lawgivers seem to attach more importance to it than justice."[2] Smith goes on to state that "Concord is the aim of lawmaking, and where friendship exists, there is already concord."[3] Macbeth, however, rejects the notion of community or communal life. He exists for himself, and by himself. Like the witches, he remains outside of society, isolated, and alone. In Act 1, Scene 7, for example, Macbeth stands outside, alone, in the dark, contemplating the murder of his king, his" kin" and his "guest," while inside people are feasting and drinking. The hospitality that Macbeth extends to the king is supposed to guarantee and ensure his safety. Yet, this intimate social and family gathering ends in a treacherous act of betrayal and murder. This one scene reveals the deep complexities of Macbeth's character, which contributes to his alienation and isolation from the rest of his community.

Similar sentiments are dramatized in Act 3, Scene 4. The appearance of Banquo's ghost triggers Macbeth's fear and guilt which disrupts the banquet, and his guests are asked to leave. Macbeth thus destroys the capacity of men to have a meal in safety and in peace. This notion is reinforced by the witches' parody of the symbolism of the shared meal in Act 4, Scene 1, in which they throw into their caldron frogs, pieces of liver, noses, lips, and aborted fetuses. Shakespeare's parody of the shared meal further underscores the importance of communal feasting in which bonds of friendship, trust, loyalty, and solidarity are formed. In dramatizing Macbeth's perversion of human relations fundamental to the stability of society, Shakespeare explores how these bonds are disrupted and destroyed by the notion of individualism and rationalism in which the individual is governed by his own ethical standards.[4]

Chivalric codes of behavior not only become a source of disempowerment for Macbeth, they also are a means whereby the masculinity of all men is measured and determined. In making Banquo the source of their misery and suffering, Macbeth suborns the murderers to kill Banquo by impugning their masculinity. He suggests that rather than defend themselves against those who oppress them, the murderers are weak and effeminate who suffer injustice in silence and fortitude by praying for those who destroy them, "Are you so gospelled, / To pray for this good man, and for his issue" (87–88). Macbeth further repudiates the murderers' masculine identity by making an analogous distinction between dogs. He suggests the murderers are essentially an inferior specimen of the male species because, unlike real men, they lack an innate killer instinct. Macbeth thus taunts the murderers as Lady Macbeth taunts him. The murderers are therefore forced to kill Banquo in order to reaffirm their masculine identity. Shakespeare reveals that heroic values are not only exploited by women, they become an avenue whereby men exploit each other.

Chivalric codes of honor become the impetus whereby paternal authority denies young men their identity, volition and autonomy. In willingly sacrificing their sons in defense of personal honor and family name, the nobility lends legitimacy to, and provides justification for, the destruction of its sons. For example, the older Siward's indifference and callousness towards the death of his young son—"Had he his hurts before?" (5.7. 88)—reveal how heroic values eclipse the intrinsic and fundamental human values of the individual. His father is not interested in the nature of his son's death, or in the manner in which he died, but rather as to whether his son had stood and fought like a man. The older Siward feels no sense of loss or waste. He has no feelings of regret that having died, his son's dreams and hopes have died with him. Instead, he rejoices that having died fighting like a man, his son has fulfilled his destiny on earth. Thomas More in *Utopia* satirizes chivalric codes of honor by having the Utopians describe honor as "nothing so much as glorie, as glory gotten in war."[5] More's irony is meant to demean heroic notions of valor to suggest that like the thousands of young men who have died in battle, there is no "glorie" in war, except loss, suffering and devastation. He implies, therefore, that patriarchy's desire to aggrandize itself from the death and suffering of its sons is, in and of itself, a violation of their intrinsic humanity.

This notion is reinforced by the older Siward's repetition of the word *worth* which ironically effaces his son's humanity in lieu of the heroic ideal. His father refuses Malcolm's attempts to honor his son for his bravery, "He's *worth* no more, / They say he parted well and paid his score" (5.7. 96–97), to suggest that his son exists solely to fulfill his father's needs and interests. Young Siward is his son, but he is more than that. He is tied irrevocably to his father, he is part of his father's inner being, reinforcing Roland Barthes' contention that the son is his father's "anteriority."[6] His son therefore has no identity, no being apart from him. The younger Siward's life belongs to and proceeds from his father. His father knows all things, sees all things and encompasses all things. All power flows from the older Siward, and returns to him.

In dramatizing the relationship between father and son, in which the role of the female is completely excised, the play articulates a notion of gender relations in which the male assumes both the paternal and maternal role. The fantasy thus dramatized by Macbeth in the first Act of the play that men are indeed "exempt from the taint of women," a notion the play finally rejects, is a fantasy germane to paternal authority and power.[7] Adelman states that "Even from the beginning of the play, the fantasy has not been Macbeth's alone: as the play's most striking bloody man, he is in the beginning the bearer of this fantasy for the all-male community that depends on his bloody prowess."[8] The play thus articulates a set of beliefs which lends credence to the notion that women have no part in the creation of men. Rather, man not only begets man, he is formed and borne by man. Man, therefore, is thus *exempt* from the fragile, weak and vulnerable nature of woman. It is this false sense of logic that the witches exploit and which ultimately contributes to Macbeth's downfall, "Be bloody, bold and resolute! / Laugh to scorn / The pow'r of man, for none of woman born / Shall harm Macbeth (4.1. 78–81). Although the nature of Macduff's caesarian birth destroys Macbeth's notions of invincibility, I submit that patriarchy's attempt to completely excise women from the world of the masculine is, in itself, an admission of the irrevocable ties that bind men to women, ties that are first forged in the womb, and that reinforce and consolidate men's relations to other men in life.

Shakespeare's critique of the heroic ideal suggests that chivalric codes of honor engender a single-mindedness that subordinates reason to passion and emotion, so that these values become distorted and contradictory. For example, Siward's unequivocal resolve: "Had I as many sons as he has hairs, / I would not wish them to a fairer death"(5.7. 1–92), suggests that these values, when given legitimacy, engender a notion of complacency and blindness so that man can no longer perceive or comprehend the truth. This is particularly evidenced in the notion that war is an extension of God's will for mankind, inherent in the older Siward's contention that having performed his duty on earth, his son is now "God's soldier." In seeking to lend Divine legitimacy to a cause which derives essentially from man's own ambition and designs, the play suggests that rather than advance the cause of mankind, heroic notions of chivalry ultimately threaten to undo those values fundamental to man's existence.

It is this extreme form of radical militarism that becomes central to humanists' repudiation of chivalric codes of honor in the sixteenth century. Influenced by a new sense of historical perspective in which events in the present could be understood in the context of the historical past, humanists unequivocally rejected aggressive militarism as antithetical to notions of civic humanism. Erasmus saw all wars as unconscionable acts against humanity, except when attacked by anti-Christian forces. In the following paragraph, Wells cites Erasmus's denunciation of Henry VIII's militaristic activities as absolute folly:

> Almost all wars between Christians have arisen from either stupidity or wickedness. Some young men, with no experience of life, inflamed by the bad examples of our forbearers told in the histories that fools have compiled from foolish documents, and then encouraged by flatterers and stimulated by lawyers and theologians, with the consent of connivance of bishops, and even at their desire—these young men, I say, go into war out of rashness rather than badness; and they learn, to the suffering of the whole world, that war is a thing to be avoided by every possible means.[9]

Honor gained in battle was now replaced by honor gain through service to the state. In keeping with humanistic emphasis on education, Thomas Elyot in *The Governor* instituted an educational system for future governing elites, underscoring the notion that true nobility lies in service to the State.[10] Influenced by humanists, moral philosophy became an important component of the curriculum of Tudor grammar schools in an effort to inculcate Christian virtues of piety and charity as a fundamental building block toward a more just society. With the introduction of programs of education for women designed by Erasmus and Vives for the betterment of wives, women proved that despite their gender, they were not devoid of scholastic aptitude. The education programs for women in the sixteenth century thus become a harbinger for the equality for women.

Moreover, with the dissolution of the feudal land system at the end of the fifteenth century and the introduction of new methods of warfare, a new code of values came into being: honor, originally constituted by blood and family ties inherent in the gentry, was now seen as an attribute ascribed to the individual.[11] According to Daniel Javitch, the publication of *The Book of the Courtier* by Baldesar Castiglione in 1528 demarcates the end of feudal aristocracy and the beginning of a new era in which chivalric values and feudal nobility were replaced by new codes of behavior enforced by absolutist states.[12] Stripped of their status and privilege they had so long enjoyed, feudal aristocrats were forced to adopt a new code of refinement and gentility in what was to be seen as a "civilizing process."[13] Castiglione's courtier became the embodiment of what is known as s*prezzatura*—the ability to do the most "artful things in the most artless manner."[14] The courtier is to display a sense of harmony and decorum. His speech is to convey a sense of his gentility and grace, devoid of artificiality and exaggeration. His elegance and grace is a visible symbol of the court.

These ideas gained greater resonance during the latter part of the 17th century when "conduct" and "good-breeding" constituted the epitome of honor. Richard Braithwaite argued that "Virtue is the greatest signal of Gentry and is rather expressed by goodness of the *person* rather the greatness of place."[15] The "well-ordered" country gentleman, the epitome of self-control and virtue, was seen as the embodiment of true nobility. Almsgiving, hospitality and an "open house," constituted the hallmarks of the virtuous landowner. In officiating as justices of the peace, the gentry legitimized public service as the new means of gaining honor.

Just as heroic notions of chivalry threaten to destroy those values fundamental to man's existence, heroic values threaten to disrupt and destabilize man's true understanding of himself. It is Shakespeare's insertion of Banquo's ghost for dramatic purposes that deconstructs chivalric notions of masculinity and exposes the anomalies inherent in patriarchy itself. The ghost's appearance is so alarming that Macbeth's inability to control himself transmutes into ill-defined terror. The rational gives way to the irrational, and Macbeth expresses his fear against his better self, despite his better judgment, and against his own desire to contain his feelings. An occasion which is meant to legitimize and affirm his new reign, becomes instead a scene of chaos and instability. Rather than a celebration of order, power, grandeur and majesty which now inhere in Macbeth as king, his fear and outbursts undermine his rational faculties. Rather than legitimize and empower him, his reaction to the ghost diminishes and disempowers him, suggesting that patriarchal norms, designed to inoculate man against fear and conscience are simplistic, unorthodox and self-defeating.

Furthermore, contrary to heroic conventions, Macbeth's reaction to the ghost suggests that his conscience is an inherent part of his being. Macbeth's attempt, therefore, to silence his conscience, to repress his better self from himself, to deceive himself from himself, "Why, so; being gone, / I am a man again" (3.4. 125–126), is an exercise in folly and self-deception. Moreover, in connecting Macbeth's actions to the supernatural, the play lends credence to the notion that contrary to man's assertions, there is a moral order to the universe and that man's actions are therefore not accorded divine dispensation, but rather man will pay for his actions, if not in this world, then in the next. The play thus evokes contemporary notions of the self engendered by the rise of Protestantism in the sixteenth century, in which subjectivity is now invested in the individual, rather than in a specific group or community. As a consequence, conscience now resides within the individual, rather than in a shared community.

While Macbeth's irrational behavior increases his vulnerability to Lady Macbeth's scorn and derision, her inability to see the ghost reinforces patriarchy's prescriptions of masculinity and simultaneously deconstructs these structures. Her representation of Macbeth's fears as having no basis in reality, as an innate medical condition over which he has no control, and as analogous to fears experienced by women on cold winter nights when stories are "handed down from women to women" (3.4. 71–77), reaffirm Macbeth's outbursts as despicable and reprehensible, antithetical to notions of heroic masculinity. In dramatizing Lady Macbeth's utter scorn of Macbeth's masculine virtue, "Are you a man?" (3.4. 68), "What! Quite unmanned in folly" (3.4. 85), Shakespeare interrogates and problematizes chivalric values to suggest that rather than affirm and validate his masculinity, heroic values destabilize man's inner coherence so that he can no longer make sense of the world and his place in it.

This becomes evident in Macduff's inability to assuage his grief on learning of the murder of his wife and children. While Malcolm's argument to take revenge sounds rational—"Dispute it like a man" (4.3. 256)—his admonition belies the destructive nature of his appeal. Macduff, however, knows full well the horrors of this truth. He has been forced to experience the brutal and vicious reality of chivalric values in the murder of his innocent wife and children whom he had left unprotected. Thus, Malcolm's admonishment does nothing to assuage Macduff's anguish. Rather than clarify his predicament, Malcolm's rebuke exacerbates and complicates Macduff's dilemma, "But, I must first feel it like a man" (4.3. 221). Shakespeare thus problematizes chivalric notions of revenge to suggest that rather than being the "medicine" that cures, heals, and restores man's "deadly grief," heroic codes of honor undermine those values that inform man's actions for good so that man can no longer differentiate between good and evil; between moral and immoral actions. This one scene therefore becomes crucial in highlighting one of the play's major themes: heroic notions of revenge are infused with a sense of irrationality that needs to be subdued by man's more civilizing attributes: mercy and justice. Shakespeare's dramatization of Macduff's dilemma provides a chilling and ominous perspective: forsake man's most innate sense of being, and his capacity to feel and express emotion, and you forsake intrinsic human values which give meaning and value to life. No longer constrained by moral or ethical imperatives, man will be thrust back to a dark primal world where only the sword will be victorious. Shakespeare thus exposes an inherent danger in heroic values, to suggest that, if given legitimacy, these values may well be the single-most threat to society and to man himself. Robert Grudin claims that "Psychologically and politically, the glorification of violence as a social virtue is but one step away from its acceptance as a means of individual enterprise" (160). This becomes a reality in Macbeth's own life.

Like Lady Macbeth, it is Macbeth's fundamental disdain for human life and human laws that constitute a transgression of his kingly powers. Having corrupted his military skills to gain the kingship, Macbeth now seeks to maintain power by destroying not only human life but all that is fundamental to human existence. In Act 1, Scene 4, for example, Lady Macbeth "pours" her demonic spirit of violence, destruction and death into Macbeth who, she feels, is *"too full of the milk of human kindness."* On becoming king, Macbeth, who has been convinced by Lady Macbeth that being a ruthless killer constitutes true manhood, "pours" the "sweet milk of concord into hell," to suggest that he rules and governs by the same demonic spirit "pour[ed]" into him by the female forces of darkness. Thus, despite his desire to establish an identity separate and independent of Lady Macbeth, Macbeth's actions for the most part come to be seen as an extension of her will. His actions, moreover, suggest that while Macbeth and Lady Macbeth have the capacity to gain power, they do not have the capacity to rule or maintain power. Shakespeare uses the imagery of clothing in Act 5, Scene 2, "now does he feel his title / Hang loose about him like a giant's robe / Upon a dwarfish thief" (5.2. 20–22), to suggest that the power of kingship is beyond the capacity of Macbeth to attain. Having usurped the kingship like a "dwarfish thief," he cannot realize the power invested in the "giant robe" of kingship because he lacks the legitimacy to rule. Moreover, the imagery of clothing "hang[ing] loose" evokes a sense of impotency and powerlessness to garner the majesty and mystical power inherent in kingship, to suggest that kings must have a greater vision; they must envision a reality beyond themselves and the present moment, to imagine a reality not as it is, but as it can be.

Macbeth, however, is the complete antithesis of kingly power. His actions envision a world in which all time, stability and order have been erased. Having sought guidance from the witches, he has forsaken reason, knowledge, and truth. As a result, his actions become irrational and chaotic: "From this moment / The very firstlings of my heart shall be / The very firstlings of my hand." (4.1. 146–148), to suggest that Macbeth will do whatever he wills; whenever he wills; and to whomever he wills. His murder of Macduff's wife and all their children, just to "make assurance doubly sure," comes to epitomize the notion of "Babylonical confusion" contained in the Homilies. The imagery evokes a king's loss of control of the body politic, which is analogous to the king's loss of reason.[16] In Elizabethan terms, Macbeth is out of control and out of bounds.

According to the metaphor of the body, as monarch, the king is the head of the body and, therefore, is synonymous with reason and sound judgment. These ideas were reiterated by James I in *The True Law of Free Monarchies*. Macbeth's mental disintegration therefore suggests that while the analogy seeks to affirm the rationality of the king as head of the body, the analogy, by its very nature, also implicitly affirms its opposite. As he mentally disintegrates, Macbeth is seen as undermining, disrupting and demystifying normative paradigms of hierarchy and order, central to the ideology that underlies the monarchy.

In making and breaking laws at will, moreover, Macbeth becomes the embodiment of the Machiavellian tyrant. The play thus gives expression to one of the most influential political texts in the sixteenth century, Niccoli Machiavelli's *The Prince*. Influenced by his own socio-political experience, Machiavelli advocated a system of government oriented to the rational self-interest of the State, overturning earlier political ideas promulgated by classical, Christian, and humanist writers. He argued in Chapter 18 of *The Prince* that "a prudent prince cannot and should not keep his word when to do so would go against his interest, or when the reasons that made him pledge it, no longer apply."[17]

According to Holinshed's historical narrative, however, Macbeth is a typical figure whose political behavior in a sense is the norm in the history that he narrates.[18] His violence and his utterly unscrupulous way of gaining and maintaining power is not unique or unusual. Macbeth, in fact, ruled for a whole decade before revealing his tyrannical bent. In making Macbeth a tyrant immediately upon his accession, and dramatizing the insidious nature of his crimes, including the murder of a child on stage, the play gives voice to arguments articulated by Scottish historians, that it is not a king's lack of legitimacy that necessitates his deposition but rather the "corrupting effects of power."[19] This is reinforced by the notion that although Macbeth has killed the king and usurped his crown, the charge laid against him is not usurpation, but tyranny.

Macbeth's mental instability becomes symbolized in the play by his divided body. In indelibly ascribing the word "tyrant" to individual parts of Macbeth's body in Act 3, Scene 4: "tyrant's head," "tyrant's grasp" and "tyrant's name," Shakespeare leads us further into the "heart of darkness," which resides not in forces exterior to man, but rather in the complexities that lie in man himself. David Norbrook contends that in cataloguing Macbeth's body parts, Shakespeare "not only imitated but revised the Senecan mode."[20] He states that Seneca used this device to indicate "the rational control of a passionate body." Norbrook argues that since Macbeth and Lady Macbeth are not given to "unruly passions," Shakespeare used this device to "[force] their bodies to carry through their calculating political stratagems."[21] Notwithstanding Norbrook's argument, I submit that Macbeth's individual body parts become a metaphor for his own mental disintegration and instability and, more importantly, for his inability to develop an integrated sense of the self which validates and reinforces life, as opposed to destroying it. This becomes manifested in the "body politic" by the shattered and disrupted bonds of human relations. Malcolm's declaration that he will "tread upon the tyrant's head, / Or wear it on my sword" (4.3. 51–52) reiterates the essential and necessary destruction of Macbeth, whose tyrannical actions emanate from his irrational, disturbed mind.

The image evoked by the "tyrant's name" comes to symbolize the evil inherent in Macbeth's own nature. According to Norbrook, the notion held by Camden that a title was "a natural sign," which reified the character of the nobleman, came to be part of a set of beliefs in sixteenth century England: "as though the names and natures of men were suitable and fatall necessities concurred herein with voluntary motion, in giving the name."[22] Camden believed that there was a direct correlation "between name and the bearer," and that "a noble name" could inspire men to accomplish "great deeds."[23] Thus, in inheriting the Thane of Cawdor, perhaps Macbeth unconsciously inherited

Macdonwald's destructive and rebellious character. Macbeth's acknowledgement that the "witches gave the Thane of Cawdor to me," implicates the witches as the source of destruction and death and suggests that, given the nature of their relationship, the witches' violent and destructive tendencies may well have been transferred to him. In the exchange between Macbeth and Young Siward in Act 5, Scene 7, Macbeth declares, "My name's Macbeth" (9), to which Young Siward replies: "Thou liest, abhorred tyrant; with my sword /I'll prove the lie thou speak'st"(12–13). The title then becomes a metonym for betrayal, murder, destruction, and death.

Inherent in the image of the "tyrant's grasp" is Macbeth's insatiable thirst for power. In analogizing tyranny to a disease whose "sole name blisters our tongue," Shakespeare gives voice to the horrendous nature of Macbeth's tyranny, which infects, destabilizes, and destroys the normal functioning of the human body and the body politic. The image accentuates with profundity the powerlessness and fear that grips a nation under siege, silencing the voices of its people. In destroying bonds of friendship, hospitality, loyalty and solidarity, Macbeth's tyranny engenders a climate of mistrust and suspicion, in which every man is seen as one's enemy. Scotland is thus no longer a place of conception, birth and natural growth, but rather a place of violence, destruction, and death, "It cannot / Be called our mother, but our grave" (4.3. 184–186). It is a place in which nothing grows and everything dies, in which "each new morn / New widows howl, new orphans cry, new sorrows / Strike heaven on the face, . . ." (4. 3. 5–7). Shakespeare's repetition of the word "new" in the words "*new* morn," "*new* widows," "*new* orphans" and "*new* sorrows" accentuates the preponderance of Macbeth's crime and his blatant contempt for human life and human laws. This is brought home with greater resonance by Macduff's utter disbelief at the loss of his entire family:

Macduff: My children too?

Ross: Wife, children servants, all
That could be found. (4.3. 243–245).

The utter horror of Macbeth's destruction underscores the notion that absolute power corrupts absolutely.[24] In appropriating Macbeth's tyranny in order to establish Macduff's true identity, Macduff's declaration that Malcolm is not "Fit to govern!/No not to live" (4,4 116–117), lends legitimacy to arguments made by Scottish historians in the sixteenth century that tyrants must be resisted and deposed. The play thus gives expression to one of the most polemic issues of the sixteenth century: the deposition of tyrants.[25]

Shakespeare thus undermines ideas of kingship promulgated by James I who argues in *The Trew Law of Free Monarchies* that rebellion against a king, even against a tyrannical ruler, can never be justified.²⁶ This notion was contained in the *Homily against Disobedience and Willful Rebellion* which postulates that since the king is God's anointed, God Himself will remove a tyrannical king. His subjects were thus exhorted to obey even a tyrannical ruler, since rebellion against a king constituted an act of rebellion against God Himself, for which man will suffer eternal damnation.²⁷

Unlike Macbeth, Malcolm is analogized to a "sovereign flower" that "drowns" and drives out the weeds of evil inherent in Macbeth's tyranny. The play thus makes an opposition between a notion of kingly power that is metaphorically "feminine" and a notion of kingly power that is metaphorically "masculine." The former derives its power from an inner force of moral virtue that affirms life and engenders peace, harmony and abundance. The latter derives its power from man's own ambition, and is imposed on man by force that engenders fear, brutality, violence, and death. The play thus illustrates that the stability and harmony of a society is dependent to a large degree on the moral disposition and well-being of its king. The fertility, abundance and harmony which underlie Duncan's kingship, for example, reify his moral virtues. As the embodiment of all the kingly virtues, Malcolm is the "doctor" who heals and restores Scotland to health. Likewise, Shakespeare's portrayal of England as a land of stability and order, reify the moral virtue and holiness of its king. In contrast to the evil of Macbeth's tyranny which destroys life, Shakespeare's portrayal offstage of Edward II's healing powers, affirm and give life, reinforcing the notion that although evil is present, its power cannot prevail, or triumph. In dramatizing these contradictions, the play underscores the overriding concern in the sixteenth century of the nature of a king's moral character and its direct relationship to the stability of his kingship. According to William C. Carroll, all three Scottish historians, John Major, Hector Boece, and George Buchanan give credence in their historical narratives to the healing powers of Edward the Confessor, thereby attesting to the importance of this issue.²⁸

While the play interrogates and challenges patriarchal power, the play also dramatizes a notion of masculine identity whose autonomy and independence derive from an inner force of stability and coherence. Banquo, for example, is a man who remains faithful to his own inner beliefs and truths, despite external temptations. Although Macbeth and Banquo both receive predictions, Macbeth feels compelled to bring the predictions to pass, while Banquo does not. Shakespeare, thus, portrays Banquo as a man who can be exposed to temptation, and perhaps even contemplate the temptation, but refuses to yield or be controlled by them. Banquo, therefore, becomes for the audience someone with whom they can identity and trust.

However, Holinshed, in his historical narrative, states that Banquo is complicit in the murder of Duncan.²⁹ In illustrating, for dramatic purposes, that

Banquo had *no* part in Duncan's murder, Shakespeare demonstrates that Banquo's role is crucial to determining the degree to which Macbeth has volition and thus the degree to which he is responsible for his choices. The play thus gives expression to one of the major issues of the sixteenth century—the question of human freedom. This became one of the greatest ontological quarrels between Erasmus and Martin Luther. Luther believed that everything existed by necessity and that man had no free will. He argued that because God was omnipotent, everything that happened was the direct result of God's will. Erasmus completely disagreed with Luther. He argued that for actions to be moral and meritorious, choices had to be freely made. Morals thus presupposed free will. Luther countered that faith, not works, was the means to salvation. Erasmus, however, drew on the philosophers of antiquity to illustrate that classical notions of truth, ethics, and divinity were in agreement with Christian truth.

Shakespeare demonstrates that chief among the values that constitute true masculinity is the virtue of prudence.[30] According to Classical philosophers, prudence is associated with astuteness, extraordinarily good judgment and the notion of *coup d'oeil*—the ability to comprehend the complexities of a situation and then to immediately act in a judicious and prudent manner.[31] Banquo, for example, refuses to meet with Macbeth to discuss the predictions since, in doing so, he would compromise his allegiance and loyalty to the king. Likewise, despite Macduff's earnest plea for help, Malcolm refuses to take Macduff at his word and instead seeks to establish his true identity. His determination to decipher appearance from reality, truth from untruth, suggests that Malcolm is not swayed by fleeting sensations, but is guided by an underlying set of moral principles. Malcolm's complete reversal upon determining the veracity of Macduff's assertions, "what I am truly / Is thine and my poor country's to command" (4.3. 146–147), suggests that he has the capacity for good judgment and wise action.

However, Shakespeare illustrates that human motivation is equivocal and ambiguous. Malcolm's appropriation of Macbeth's tyranny, for example, suggests that there is no guarantee that good kings will *not* become tyrants. Moreover, although Macduff is seen as the instrument of God's retribution, Malcolm questions his honor and his personal integrity in leaving his family unprotected. In the previous scene, his wife questions his love and commitment. Furthermore, Shakespeare's portrayal of Macduff as politically expedient, in his attempt to enjoin Malcolm to return to Scotland, is troubling. Macduff sees nothing wrong in young women becoming victims of Malcolm's supposed lust, which he states has "no bottom, none, / In my voluptuousness: your wives, your daughters, / Your matrons and your maids, could not fill up / The cistern of my lust" (4.3. 69–73). Macduff's argument that Malcolm can convey the pretense of virtue and still pursue his lust in private is a particularly chilling Machiavellian perspective. He sees nothing wrong in Malcolm's desire to cheat nobles out of their land, steal their wealth, and willing concedes all Scotland's resources to satisfy Malcolm's "stanchless avarice" (89). Shakespeare suggests that despite man's need for an absolute and moral understanding of the world, this is attenuated by human motivation which is more obscure and ambiguous than we might think.

Shakespeare's interrogation of manhood throughout the play thus gives voice to the emergence of a new conception of man in the Renaissance. Unlike medieval thought which held that man's position in the world is immutable, fixed and unchanging, humanists in the sixteenth century celebrated man's individuality and his boundless potential. According to Martin Wiggins in *Shakespeare and the Drama of His Time*,[32] it is *Hamlet*, in the following soliloquy, who gives expression to the humanistic understanding of man: "What a piece of work is a man! how noble in reason, how infinite in faculty, in form and moving how express and admirable, in action how like an angel, in apprehension how like a god: the beauty of the world, the paragon of animals . . . "[33] Shakespeare's hymn of praise, "What a piece of work is a man!" celebrates man as the highest form of God's creation, surpassing all other creatures on earth. Humanists believed man's potential was *infinite*—that man could reach the heights of perfection, and that his capacity for comprehension and understanding were without limit or constraint. It is man's reason, however, that lends "nobility" to his endeavors, enabling him to comprehend the breadth, width and depth of the universe and thus unlock its mysteries. Humanists believed, moreover, that while man could aspire to, and achieve the perfection of "a god," he could also degenerate to the ranks of the beasts and become "the paragon of animals."

In this Chapter, I have demonstrated that patriarchy's prescriptions of gender not only constitute masculine identity, they simultaneously undermine and disempower that identity; an ideology that affirms man's power and authority, simultaneously is the source of man's disempowerment and destruction. The play thus articulates a process of subjectification in which men are seen as authors of their actions, and at the same time are restricted and constrained by forces beyond their control.[34] However, in dramatizing that notions of masculine identity dramatized throughout the play are, for the most part, unstable and incoherent, the play suggests that Shakespeare is critical of the patriarchal system itself. That is, in predicating masculine identity on a discourse of gendered difference, heroic notions of masculinity shape a masculine identity that falsifies man's true understanding of himself and that, in turn, limits his ability to achieve his potential. The play thus interrogates patriarchy's notions of masculine identity to suggest that perhaps the system serves as a function of expediency rather than a manifestation of an innate truth.

NOTES

1. Smith 61.
2. Smith 61.
3. Smith 61.
4. In dramatizing these conflicts, Shakespeare exposes opposing political viewpoints prevalent during the 16th Century. Donald R. Kelley in "Elizabethan Political Thought" argues that "In general, European political thought in the 16th Century drew upon two major resources—Aristotelian philosophy, 'practical' as well as 'theoretical,' and Roman jurisprudence, which included canon and some parts of feudal as well as civil law." The former, inherent in James I's political beliefs, is a system of government grounded in common law with its appeal to tradition and the continuity of institutions. Hence, the Reformation was seen as return to the original church handed down by the monarch. This contrasted strongly with George Buchanan and his Scottish contemporaries, whose political worldview was grounded more in the "rationalistic" Roman civil laws. According to David Norbrook, "Scotland did not have a full equivalent of the English common law, and the language of tradition did not play such an important part in Scottish political discourse." The Reformation, therefore, provoked anti-monarchy sentiments, which gave rise to a even greater "pride" in their own Scottish traditions (Norbrook 114).
5. Thomas More, *Utopia,* trans. and ed. Robert M. Adams, 2nd ed. (London: Norton, 1992), 19.
6. Roland Barthes, *On Racine* qtd. in Kahn 48.
7. Adelman 141.
8. Adelman 141.
9. qtd in Wells 13.
10. Thomas Elyot, *The Boke Named The Governor* (London: J.M. Dent & Co, 1531), 69.
11. Foyster 33.
12. Daniel Javitch, Preface in *The Book of the Courtier*, by Baldesar Castiglione (New York: WW Norton 2002) viii.
13. Javitch viii.
14. Harry Berger, Jr., "Sprezzatura and the Absence of Grace" in Baldesar Castiglione, *The Book of the Courtier,* (New York: WW Norton 2002), 295.
15. Foyster 35.
16. As Macbeth mentally disintegrates, the play gives expression to one of the greatest social issues in the Renaissance: the notion of madness. Unlike modern practices, medicine and psychiatry in the sixteenth century were constituted as one branch of study in which the body became the site of both physical and mental disorders. Madness in the Renaissance thus was understood in terms of the humoral theory. Tim-

othy Bright in his *Treatise on Melancholy* defined madness in terms of Natural and Unnatural Melancholy. In vacillating between extreme emotions of "love, hatred, hope and fear," Macbeth suffers from Natural melancholy. At the same time, in becoming a murderer and an infanticide because he feels he has been cheated out of establishing a dynasty, Macbeth's "bitter enmity" suggests that he suffers from Unnatural melancholy. As such, according to Bright, Macbeth fate is sealed. He cannot be cured and suffers the eternal agony of the damned. He states, "Here no medicine, no purgation, no cordiall, no tryacle or balme are able to assure the afflicted soule."

17. Machiavelli 48.

18. Alan Sinfield argues that perhaps "For the Jamesian reading, it is necessary to feel that Macbeth is distinctively 'evil.'" He goes on to point out, however, that although Macbeth is "a murderer and an oppressive ruler," he is not, as we see in Holinshed, the "polar opposite" but indeed 'one version" of an absolute monarch (Sinfield 124).

19. David Norbrook contends that in having Macbeth become a tyrant simultaneous with his accession to the throne, Shakespeare seems to suggest that "bad rule follows inevitably from lack of legitimacy" (Norbrook 96). However, he argues that as is evident from historical narratives, what becomes important to Scottish historians is the "corrupting effects of power" and the necessity that tyrants be removed (Norbrook 96).

20. Norbrook 113.

21. Norbrook 113.

22. Norbrook 109–110.

23. Norbrook 110.

24. *Macbeth* reiterates ideas held by Scottish historian George Buchanan who argued that the powers of kings were not absolute. In his essay, "Materialist Shakespeare," Alan Sinfield states: "Arguments in favor of absolutism constitute one part of Macbeth's ideological field - the range of ideas and attitudes brought into play by the text; another main part may be represented by Buchanan's De jure regni (1579) and History of Scotland (1582)." (Sinfield 82). For Buchanan, tyrannicide was a "heroic act" that rescued "public rationality" from the evils of "private passion" (Norbrook 92). Like the ancient Greeks, Buchanan sought to underscore the significance of this event by memorializing the tyrannicide of Mary, Queen of Scots in the issuance of a coin (Norbrook 92). The inscription on the coin: (if I deserve it the blade will be used in my defense. If not, it will be turned against me), reiterated his belief that sovereignty derived from the people and therefore the people had the right to overthrow tyrants. (Norbrook 92). In "The Powers of the Crown in Scotland," Buchanan asserts that all kings "swear obedience to the laws" and their continued reign was contingent on that obedience (Buchanan 56).

25. According to W.C. Carroll, resistance to tyrants was established in Europe in the context of religious civil wars between Protestants and Catholics, well before the reign of the Stuart kings. Central to this discourse was the argument made by the Huguenots that monarchical governments had adopted Machiavelli's theory of government as a basis for governance. Thus, in 1579 Stephano Junio Bruot Celta argued in his most famous text, *A Defense of Liberty against Tyrants* that kings could be

resisted both for "breaking the law of God and His church" and for "suppressing his people." Tyranny was therefore resisted both on political and religious grounds. See W.C. Carroll, ed. *William Shakespeare's Macbeth: Texts and Context*, (London:Macmillan Press Ltd., 1999), 44.

26. According to Norbrook, James I repudiated all of Buchanan's theories that subjects had the right to depose a tyrant and stated they must endure even a tyrannical king (Norbrook 93). Despite James I's attempt to abolish Buchanan's historical writings, Norbrook argues that they became the "most widely read book in the covenanting armies" and frequently cited after the deposition and murder of his son, Charles (Norbrook 93).

27. Alan Sinfield in his essay *"Macbeth: History, Ideology and Intellectuals,"* argues that the distinctions made by James I between "a lawfully good king" and a "usurping tyrant," outlined in his work "Basilikon Doron," falls apart, even by his own analysis. In ascribing to himself a duly sanctioned mandate to rule, the "lawful king" precludes the possibility of public scrutiny and the derision of his subjects, since all bad acts executed against him are now seen as acts committed against God Himself (Sinfield 13). The definition, moreover, excludes the possibility that a good king may become a tyrant. As Sinfield points out, James I's definition falls apart even here since Mary, Queen of Scots is a "lawful ruler" who also becomes a tyrant. Furthermore, in making the distinction contingent on motive, rather than behavior, James' definition legitimizes the violent and tyrannical actions of a good king, made in the name of the State, as not only essential but legitimate (Sinfield 13).

28. William C.Carroll, ed .*Macbeth: Texts and Contexts* (New York: Bedford/St. Martin, 1999).

29. Raphael Holinshed, from *The Chronicles of England, Scotland and Ireland* in *William Shakespeare's Macbeth: Texts and Contexts* (The Bedford Shakespeare Series) ed. W.C. Carroll (London: Macmillan Press Ltd., 1999), 143.

30. Montesquieu asserts that the origins of political greatness lay in "prudence, wisdom and perseverance" since prudence would "guard the passions of individuals for the sake of order and guard the guardians for the sake of freedom" (556). See Montesquieu. *Considerations on the Causes of the Romans' Greatness and Decline*, trans. David Lowenthal. (London: Collier-Macmillan, 1965), 556.

31. Aristotle, *Nicomachean Ethics*, Book Six, Chapters 11 and 12, trans. J.A.K. Thomson (London: Allen and Unwin, 1953).

32. Martin Wiggins, *Shakespeare and the Drama of His Time* (Oxford: Oxford University Press, 2000), 49.

33. William Shakespeare's, *The Tragedy of Hamlet*, ed. Sylvan Barnet, 2nd ed. (New York: Penguin Putman, Inc., 1998). 2.2 305–9.

34. I have taken this definition of subjectification from Louis Montrose's *The Elizabethan Subject and the Spensarian Text* in which he explicates the dialectical relationship between subject and state as "a process of subjectification that, on the one hand, shapes individuals as loci of consciousness and initiators of actions; and on the other, positions, motivates and constrains them with networks of power beyond their comprehension or control" (Montrose 306).

Chapter V

Elements of Tragedy

Like historians, dramatists during the 16th Century sought to impose a shape to their dramatic narratives.[1] By selecting only those events in a king's reign that dealt with tyranny, corruption, or abuse of power, dramatists could portray the fall of kings or personages of high rank from a place of honor and majesty to a place of great depth, and their ultimate destruction and death by their own actions. This gave rise to the genre of tragedy with the successful production in 1561 of the first English tragedy.[2] Shakespeare's selection of events in the latter part of Macbeth's reign, in which his tyrannical bent is manifested, permits Shakespeare to shape the play into a tragedy, *The Tragedy of Macbeth*. In so doing, Shakespeare explores the psychology of power during Macbeth's reign and the political ramifications of his actions that lead to his demise.

Shakespearean tragedy, therefore, serves an important social function. In dramatizing Macbeth as both the hero and the villain, Shakespeare humanizes Macbeth's experience, thus allowing the audience to identity with him and thus experience his anguish and torment. In so doing, the audience can vicariously engage in criminal behavior and experience the process of purging those feelings, and in the end assent to the justice of his destruction.

Yet, the closure of play becomes very problematic. The necessary destruction of Macbeth and his refusal to repent complicates our understanding of Macbeth as the tragic hero, and signals yet again that sense of moral ambivalence and uncertainty that resonates throughout the play. For Malcolm, Macbeth is a far cry from a tragic hero: "this dead butcher and his fiend like Queen" (5.7. 115). His view of Macbeth as an abomination to be rooted out and killed before any sense of civility can return creates a dilemma for the audience who must in some way identify with the Macbeth, if the play, as a tragedy, is to fulfill its objective.

Malcolm's sentiment finds resonance in Samuel Johnson's commentary on *Macbeth.* Writing in the eighteenth century, Dr. Johnson suggests that the Macbeths have no redeeming qualities and their actions have earned them nothing but disdain. He states "This play is deservedly celebrated for the propriety of its fictions, and solemnity, grandeur, and variety of action; but it has no nice discriminations of character, the events are too great to admit the influence of particular dispositions . . . Their passions are directed to their true end. Lady Macbeth is merely detested; and though the courage of Macbeth preserves some esteem, yet every reader rejoices at his fall."[3] Dr. Johnson suggests that the Macbeths are antithetical to all notions of moral goodness.

However, Shakespearean scholar, A.C. Bradley, asserts that Shakespeare's tragic heroes are not ordinary men, of ordinary stature or consequence. On the contrary, they are men whose extraordinary acts of valor and feats of courage constitute a sense of greatness "that in real life we have known scarcely anyone resembling them"[4] As a result, their fall from a place of high standing defies conventional morality and inspires not moral condemnation, but rather awe, wonder, and fear. Bradley suggests that tragedy, by its very nature, precludes moral judgment that inheres in traditional morality. Of the Macbeths, he states, "These two characters are fired by one and the same passion of ambition; and to a considerable extent they are alike. The disposition of each is high, proud, and commanding. They are born to rule, if not to reign. And if, as time goes on, they drift a little apart, they are the fruitlessness of their ambition. They remain to the end tragic, even grand?[5] Unlike Dr. Johnson, Bradley implies that Macbeth's ability to look death in the face and defy its power, constitutes an act of heroic valor that is sublime and majestic, even "grand." This notion is reinforced by T. McAlindon who argues that, "violent death is one of the tests of heroic authenticity, the event which above all others can give meaning and value."[6]

Yet, while the audience accedes to Macbeth's necessary death, Macbeth's lack of repentance denies the play from reaching full closure. Unlike Macbeth's defiance, the repentance of the traitor Macdonwald at the beginning of the play restores a sense of moral order to the universe. In acknowledging his crimes against the king and imploring his forgiveness, Macdonwald's repentance "nothing in his life / Became him like the leaving it;" (1.4. 6–9), becomes the catalyst that heals and reconciles a society marred by the affects of violence and destruction. T. McAlindon states that "so important is the motif of forgiveness that it often extends beyond the death of the protagonist to form the basis of social reintegration or—a key word and stage image—'joining.'" It is an unequivocal acknowledgement that in a moral universe, evil cannot prevail and that in the end, good triumphs over evil.

Unlike Macdonwald, Macbeth's defiance and refusal to repent, "I will not yield /To kiss the ground before young Malcolm's feet /And to be baited with the rabble's curse / Before my body / I throw my warlike shield: lay on Macduff, /And damned be he that first cries 'Hold, enough'"(5.7. 67–74), destabilizes the very foundation of the moral universe and undermines the laws from which the stability of society derive. His defiance suggests that a culture that glorifies and perpetuates violence inevitably corrupts those principles which define and give shape to a system of values so that man's moral understanding of the universe is more obscure and equivocal. This is particularly manifested in Act 1, Scene 2, in which Shakespeare dramatizes the dialectical relationship between Macbeth as the resolute, predatory and fearless "man of action" and Duncan as the refined and virtuous king who extols Macbeth's savagery.

Shakespeare's use of the word "Golgotha" evokes the horror of man's inhumanity to man, encapsulated in the image of "reeking wounds" which reduce the battlefield to a sea of blood. In analogizing Macbeth's actions to Christ's crucifixion, Shakespeare suggests that unlike Christ who died to redeem man from death, sin, and evil, Macbeth's butchery reduces man to human carnage, devoid of human value and human dignity. Macbeth is not only interested in killing his enemies, he is determined to desecrate their humanity as he "carves out his passage" and "unseams" the traitor Macdonwald from "the nave to the chops" (1.2. 19–22). Duncan's exhalation, moreover, of Macbeth's barbaric and savage butchery: "O, valiant cousin! worthy gentleman"(1.2. 26), belies his own virtuous and noble character. As a result the means (savage brutality and violence) and the ends (peace and justice) are no longer seen as two separate and distinct entities, but rather become irretrievably fused and enmeshed so that the values that govern and underlie men's actions no longer provide moral clarity. In his essay *Shakespeare After Theory,* David Scott Kastan argues that "Macbeth's violent defense of the king at once confirms Duncan's rule and collapses the distinction upon which it rests. Difference dissolves into disruptive similarity. Hero and villain, as Harry Berger has ingeniously demonstrated are disturbingly intertwined and indistinguishable."[7]

A similar fusion of values is seen in the last scene of the play when Macduff hands Malcolm the decapitated head of Macbeth: "Hail King! for so thou art. Behold where stands / Th'usurper's cursed head: the time is free" (5.7. 98–99). Malcolm's response is with filled gracious simplicity and hospitality. His use of the words "loves," "friends," and "home" evoke a celebratory tone of restoration, order and civility. His invocation of the "grace of Grace" implies the kingship is now under the direction of, and guided by, a Divine Power, "What's more to do, / Which would be planted newly with the time,

/As calling home our exiled friends abroad . . . / That calls upon us, by the grace of Grace / We will perform in measure, time, and pace: / So thanks to all at once, and to each one, / Whom we invite to see us crowned at Scone" (4.7. 110–121). In dramatizing this contradiction, Shakespeare problematizes heroic values which legitimize and provide justification for the use of barbaric force and savagery to suggest that in the pursuit of an even greater principle, moral values themselves become compromised. Shakespeare refuses to give us any easy answers. He provides no solution to the problem he dramatizes. Macbeth's refusal to repent thus provokes issues far greater and more profound which are beyond the scope of the play to address.

Yet, things do not change when Macbeth is finally destroyed. Notions of heroic masculinity remain alive and well. As Shakespeare dramatizes, in leading Malcolm's army against Macbeth and destroying him, Macduff assumes the role played by Macbeth in the beginning of the play, to suggest that in corrupting his military skills, Macbeth's actions are not the *cause*, but the *effect*, of a system in which men are seen as representatives or "products" of a society, and not the creators of evil.[8]

NOTES

1. Challenged by humanists to adapt a more rigorous historical narrative that focused on the dynamics of political behavior of those in power, historians during the Renaissance turned to the historical writings of Tacitus whose works were first translated and published by Henry Savile in 1591. Tacitus focused on the ruthless, predatory nature of politics at the center of monarchial power. He illustrated that despite the providential view of history, monarchial power was not fixed or immutable, but was subject to social and cultural change and that the decline of moral virtue could subvert and destroy laws fundamental and essential to the monarchy. Renaissance historiography, which informed Shakespeare's plays, therefore, took a more complex and political stance. History was no longer seen to be a narrative of past events. Rather, historians sought to impose a shape to historical events that engendered a political and philosophical vision. Historical events therefore were now being understood through the actions and motivations of those at the center of power, rather than, in the words of Louis Montrose, the ineluctable "working out of Divine Providence."

2. *Gorboduc*—also known as *Ferrex and Porrex*—is considered the first successful English tragedy in the Senecan style. Written by Thomas Sackville and Thomas Norton in 1561, the play illustrates the complete destruction and death of Gorbodoc's entire family which occurs as a direct result of the king's determination to divide his kingdom between his two sons, thereby overturning the line of monarchical succession.

3. Samuel Johnson, "*Macbeth*" in *William Shakespeare's Macbeth* (London: Penguin Books Ltd, 1998), 129.

4. A.C. Bradley, *From Shakespearean Tragedy* in *Approaches to Macbeth*. ed. Jay L. Halio (California: Wadsworth Publishing Company, Inc., 1966) 15.

5. A.C. Bradley, *From Shakespearean Tragedy* in *William Shakespeare's Macbeth* (London: Penguin Books Ltd, 1998), 34.

6. T. McAlindon 48.

7. David Scott Kaston, *Shakespeare After Theory* (New York and London: Routledge, 1999), 3.

8. A.C. Bradley argues that in Shakespeare's tragedies, evil exists in the "moral order" or system, and is produced by it. He states: "We do not think of Hamlet merely as failing to meet its demand, of Antony as merely sinning against it, or even of Macbeth as simply attacking it. What we feel corresponds quite as much to the ideas that they are *its* parts, expressions and products; that in their defect or evil *it* is untrue to its soul of goodness, and falls into conflict and collision with itself . . ." (24). Bradley suggests that the inherent flaws of Hamlet, Antony and Macbeth are *not* the causes of evil, but rather that these tragic heroes are "products" or representatives of a system which is in "conflict" with itself, because the system itself has digressed from its innate tendency towards "goodness."

Chapter VI

Conclusion

I think it is fair to say that Shakespeare accepted the general conventions of patriarchy. However, his critique of the heroic ideal suggests that he did not accept heroic values unreservedly. First, the play suggests that Shakespeare was highly skeptical of the extreme nature of gender polarities which imposed on man a fundamentally false understanding of himself and which, in turn, permitted women to undermine and invalidate their masculine identity. Secondly, the play demonstrates that although chivalric codes of honor are imbued with a sense of irrationality, it is the destructive nature of its appeal on the masculine psyche that is most disturbing and dangerous. Shakespeare is thus provocative in his dramatization of moral, ethical and political problems which beset the characters in the play: how does a society which glorifies and perpetuates violence, define or shape a system of values? To what extent do heroic values corrupt or undermine those values? Can heroic values truly be an avenue to achieving peace? Although Shakespeare provides no solution to these problems, the play does demonstrate that, if corrupted, heroic notions of masculinity could, in effect, destroy entire cultures or societies.

Thus, I contend that central to Shakespeare's understanding of true manhood is the notion that the masculine ideal is, first and foremost, a man of tempered action and moderation. His greatness derives not from his physical prowess, but rather from a sense of moral courage that tempers his acts of courage and valor with mercy and justice. The play thus articulates a notion of ideal masculinity in which man learns to subdue the arts of warfare with the more civilizing aspects of human behavior. Both Macbeth and Banquo, for example, are men of formidable physical prowess, but it is Banquo who realizes in Macbeth his most deepest fears, "There is none but he / Whose being I do fear, and under him / My genius is rebuked" (3.1. 54–56). Macbeth's apprehension arises from the knowledge that despite the temptation to do so, Banquo cannot be corrupted. Unlike Macbeth, Banquo's actions are not governed by vain or glorious desires or feats, but rather are guided by wisdom and equanimity, enabling him to remain steadfast to those principles which give meaning and value to life.

At a period in history when the concept of manhood and human greatness was a matter of intense debate, William Shakespeare's *The Tragedy of Macbeth* represents a complex critique of the dangers inherent in heroic notions of masculinity.

Works Cited

Adelman, Janet. *Suffocating Mothers: Fantasies of Maternal Origin in Shakespeare's Plays,* Hamlet *to* The Tempest. New York: Routledge, 1992.
Alfar, Cristina Leon. *Fantasies of Female Evil: The Dynamics of Gender and Power in Shakespearean Tragedy.* Newark: U of Delaware P, 2003.
Anderson, Ruth Leila. *Elizabethan Psychology and Shakespeare's Plays.* New York: Russell, 1966.
Aristotle. *The Art of Rhetoric.* Trans. H. C. Lawson-Tancred. London: Penguin, 1991.
———. *Nicomachean Ethics.* Bk. 6, Chap. 11, 12. Trans. J. A. K. Thomson. London: Allen and Unwin, 1953.
Berger, Harry, Jr. "Sprezzatura and the Absence of Grace." *The Book of the Courtier.* By Baldesar Castiglione. New York: Norton, 2002. 295–307.
Bradley, A. C. "From Shakespearean Tragedy." *William Shakespeare's* Macbeth. London: Penguin, 1998. 130–44.
———. "The Substance of Shakespearean Tragedy." *Approaches to* Macbeth. Ed. Jay L. Halio Belmont, CA: Wadsworth, 1966. 10–25.
Breitenberg, Mark. *Anxious Masculinity in Early Modern England.* Cambridge Studies in Renaissance Literature and Culture 10. Cambridge: UP, 1996.
Buchanan, George. "The Powers of the Crown in Scotland." *William Shakespeare's* Macbeth: *Texts and Contexts.* The Bedford Shakespeare Series. Ed. W. C. Carroll. London: Macmillan, 1999. 242–43.
Carroll, W. C., ed. *William Shakespeare's* Macbeth: *Texts and Context.* The Bedford Shakespeare Series. London: Macmillan, 1999.
Castiglione, Baldesar. *The Book of the Courtier: An Authoritative Text and Criticism.* Ed. Daniel Javitch. New York: Norton, 2002.
Elyot, Thomas. *The Boke Named The Governor.* London: Dent, 1531.
Foucault, Michel de. "The History of Sexuality." *The Critical Tradition.* Ed. David H. Richter. 2nd ed. Boston: Bedford, 1998. 1045–65.
Foyster, Elizabeth A. *Manhood in Early Modern England: Honor, Sex and Marriage.* London: Longman, 1999.

Holinshed, Raphael. "The Chronicles of England, Scotland and Ireland." *William Shakespeare's* Macbeth: *Texts and Contexts.* The Bedford Shakespeare Series. Ed. W. C. Carroll. London: Macmillan, 1999. 135–50.

——. "The Chronicles of England, Scotland and Ireland." in William Shakespeare's *The Tragedy of Macbeth.* Ed. Sylvan Barnet. 2nd ed. London: Penguin, 1998. 104–120

James, I. "The True Law of Free Monarchies." *William Shakespeare's* Macbeth: *Texts and Contexts.* The Bedford Shakespeare Series. Ed. W. C. Carroll. London: Macmillan, 1999. 213–20.

Javitch, Daniel. Preface. *The Book of the Courtier.* By Baldesar Castiglione. New York: Norton, 2002. vii–xvi

Johnson, Samuel. *Macbeth. William Shakespeare's* Macbeth. London: Penguin, 1998. 121–29.

Kahn, Coppelia. *Man's Estate: Masculine Identity in Shakespeare.* Berkeley: U of California P, 1981.

Kastan, David Scott. *Shakespeare after Theory.* New York: Routledge, 1999.

Kelly, Donald R. "Elizabethan Political Thought." *The Varieties of British Political Thought, 1500–1800.* Ed. J. G. A. Pocock. Cambridge: UP, 1997. 48–79.

Lacan, Jacques. "The Meaning of the Phallus." *Feminine Sexuality: Jacques Lacan and the Ecole Freudienne.* Trans. Jacqueline Rose. Ed. Juliet Mitchell and Jacqueline Rose. New York: Norton, 1982. 60–80.

Machiavelli, Niccolo. *The Prince.* Trans. and ed. Robert M. Adams. 2nd ed. New York: Norton, 1992.

McAlindon, T. *English Renaissance Tragedy.* Vancouver: U of British Columbia P, 1986.

Montesquieu. *Considerations on the Causes of the Romans' Greatness and Decline.* Trans. David Lowenthal. London: Collier-Macmillan, 1965.

Montrose, Louis. *The Purpose of Playing.* Chicago: U of Chicago P, 1996.

——. "Shaping Fantasies: Figurations of Gender and Power in Elizabethan Culture." *Representing the English Renaissance.* Ed. Stephen Greenblatt. Berkeley: U of California P, 1988. 31–64.

——. "The Elizabethan Subject and the Spenserian Text," in *Literary Theory/Renaissance Texts,* Eds. Patricia Parker and David Quint. Baltimore and London: The John Hopkins University Press, 1986. 303–340.

More, Thomas. *Utopia.* Trans. and ed. Robert M. Adams. 2nd ed. London: Norton, 1992.

Norbrook, David. "Macbeth and the Politics of Historiography." *Politics of Discourse.* Ed. Kevin Sharpe and Steven N. Zwicker. Berkeley: U of California P, 1987. 78–116.

Ovid. *Metamorphoses.* Trans. Rolfe Humphries. Indianapolis: Indiana UP, 1983. 234–38.

Richter, Melvin. *Selected Political Writings.* Indianapolis: Hackett, 1990.

Rubin, Gayle. "The Traffic in Women: Notes toward a 'Political Economy' of Sex." *Toward an Anthropology of Women.* Ed. Rayna R. Rieter. New York: Monthly Review P, 1975. 157–210.

Scaliger, J. C. "Rhetoric and Poetics." *The Cambridge History of Renaissance Philosophy*. Ed. Quentin Skinner and Eckhard Kessler. New York: Cambridge UP, 1988. 715–745.
Shakespeare, William. *Macbeth.* Simply Shakespeare. New York: Barron's, 2002.
———. *The Tragedy of Hamlet.* Ed. Sylvan Barnet. 2nd ed. New York: Penguin, 1998.
———. *The Tragedy of Macbeth.* Ed. Sylvan Barnet. 2nd ed. London: Penguin, 1998.
Sinfield, Alan. "*Macbeth*: History, Ideology and Intellectuals." *William Shakespeare's* Macbeth. Ed. Alan Sinfield. New York: St. Martin's P, 1992. 121–35.
Smith, Bruce R. *Shakespeare and Masculinity.* Oxford: Oxford UP, 2000.
Vickers, Brian. "Rhetoric and Poetics." *The Cambridge History of Renaissance Philosophy*. Ed. Quentin Skinner and Eckhard Kessler. New York: Cambridge UP, 1988. 715–45.
Wells, Robin Headlam. *Shakespeare on Masculinity.* Cambridge: UP, 2000.
Wiggins, Martin. *Shakespeare and the Drama of His Time.* Oxford: Oxford UP, 2000.

Index

Adelman, Janet, 7, 10n4, 10n10, 21, 32n7, 32n8
Alfar, Cristina, 8, 9, 10, 12, 18
Aristotle, 8, 10n9, 13, 19, 32, 34; Art of Rhetoric, 3–4n7, 13, 17n6, 17n7; Nicomachean Ethics, 34n31

Banquo, 20, 29, 30, 40, 41
Barthes, Roland, 21, 32n6
Berger, Harry Jr., 32n14, 37
Body: anatomical difference, 3, 5, 17, 18, 31; female, 3, 5, 7–11, 13–15, 17–19, 21, 25; Galenic theories of the, 5; heat, 5, 7; male, 2, 3, 5, 7–11, 13–15, 17–20, 25; metaphor of the, 13, 26, 27, 29
Bradley, A. C., 36, 39n4, 39n5, 39n8
Braithwaite, Richard, 23
Breitenberg, Mark, 9, 9n2, 10n14, 16, 17, 18n13, 18n19
Bright, Timothy, 33n16

Camden, 27
Carroll, William C., 29, 33n25, 34n28, 34n29
Castiglione, Baldesar, 23, 32n12, 32n14
child, 14–16, 27
children, 14, 15, 24, 25, 26, 28, 34

chivalric: behavior, 20, 23; codes, 20–23, 25, 40; honor, 2, 20–23, 25, 40
chivalry, 2, 22, 23
class purity, 9
conscience, 8, 24
crucifixion, 37

Duncan, 12, 14, 16, 19, 29, 37

early modern period, 2, 3, 5, 8, 9, 12, 14, 16, 17, 19
Elizabethan culture, 1, 2, 10, 10n9, 37
Elyot, Thomas, 23, 32n10
England, Elizabethan, 1, 3, 7, 9, 9n2, 12, 16, 17n1, 18n14, 27, 29, 34n29
Erasmus, 22, 23, 30
Eve, as in Adam and Eve, 12, 15

Father, 1, 2, 16, 21
father-son relationship, 21
female, 3, 5, 7–9, 10n11, 10n15, 11, 13, 14, 15, 17, 18n10, 19, 21, 25; body, 8, 10n15; chastity, 9; evil, 8, 10n11; nature, 7; sexuality, 3, 9
feminine desire, 3, 11, 12, 13, 15, 17
Foucault, Michel de, 18n12
Foyster, Elizabeth A., 8, 14

gender: difference, 11, 16; polarities, 7, 14, 40; prescription, 7, 17; relations, 8, 21; reversal, 7, 16; roles, 7, 16
Golgotha, 37
Gorboduc, 38n2
Gouge, William, 11
Grudin, Robert, 25

Hamlet, 1, 3n2, 31, 34, 39
Henry VIII, 22
historians: George Buchanan, 29, 32n4, 33n24; Hector Boece, 29; John Major, 29; Scottish, 27–29, 32, 33n19, 33n24
Holinshed, Raphael, 16, 18n14, 27, 29, 33n18
homilies, 26
Homily Against Disobedience and Willful Rebellion, 29
humanist, 2, 13, 22, 23, 26, 31, 38n1
humors, 5, 7, 17, 32n16; imbalance of humors, 10, 17, 18

individualism, 20

James I as in The True Law of Free Monarchies, 26, 28, 32n4, 34n26, 34n27
Javitch, Daniel, 23
Johnson, Samuel, 36

Kastan, David Scott, 37
Kelley, Donald R., 32n4
Khan, Coppelia, 4

Lacan, 17n10; phallic power, 18; phallus, 17
Lady Macbeth: betrayal, 12; desire, 11, 15, 16; Eve, 12, 15; frightening figure, 11, 15; Machiavelli, 10, 12, 17; resolute, 6, 11, 16, 22; serpent, 12; unwavering, 16

Macbeth: infanticide, 15, 33; infantilization, 16; tyrant, 27, 28, 30, 33, 34
Macduff, 13, 22, 24–26, 28, 30, 37, 38
Machiavelli, Niccolo, as in The Prince, 10n6, 17n4, 26, 33n17
Machiavellian tyrant, 26
Male: bonds, 12, 13, 19, 20, 27; friendships, 13, 19, 20, 28; reason, 3n7, 2,13, 14, 16, 22, 26, 31
manhood: virtu and fortune, 10n6; will and action, 12, 15
masculine: autonomy, 1, 2, 15, 19, 20, 29; disempowered, 3, 12, 20, 24, 31; heroic, 1, 2, 3, 7, 11, 12, 15, 16, 21–25, 31, 33, 35–41; heroic ideal, 1, 2, 7, 11, 21, 22, 40; heroic masculinity, 1, 7, 16, 24, 38; identity, 1–5, 7, 9, 11, 13, 16, 17, 19–21, 29, 31, 40; impotence, 14–16, 26; independence, 1, 15, 19, 25, 29; virtue, 1, 5–7, 14, 15, 19, 23, 24, 29, 30, 31, 38n1
McAlindon, A., 13, 17n2, 36, 39n6
Montrose, Louis in The Elizabethan Subject and Spensarian Text, 10n9, 34n34, 38n1
More, Thomas in Utopia, 21, 32n5

Norbrook, David, 27, 32n4, 33n19, 33n24, 34n26

Orgel, 7, 10n3, 17
Orpheus, 13
Ovid, 17n8

Patriarchy: authority, 5, 8; fears, 3, 9, 12; power, 7, 8, 11, 14; sovereignty, 2, 33n24
persuasion, 11–13
Protestant, 2, 24, 33
puritan, 2, 11

radical militarism, 22
rationalism, 20
Renaissance, 2, 7, 10n2, 10n6, 10n9, 12, 13, 17n2, 17n9, 31, 32n16, 38n1
Renaissance mythography, 13
repent/repentance, 3, 35–38
restoration, 37
roles: paternal, 31, 40; maternal, 10, 15, 16; polarity, 5, 7, 14, 40; transgression of, 11; reversal of, 7, 16

Scaliger, J. C., 13, 17n9
Sexuality: difference, 3, 5, 17; female, 3, 9, 18
Sinfield, Alan, 33n18, 33n24, 34n27
Siward, 21, 28
Smith, Bruce R., 2, 3n4, 7, 19
St. Augustine, 13
Stone, Lawrence, 2

The Book of the Courtier. *See* Baldesar Castiglione
The Elizabethan Subject and Spensarian Text. *See* Louis Montrose
The Law's Resolutions of Women's Rights, 12
tragedy, 3, 35, 36, 38n2
Treatise of Melancholy. *See* Timothy Bright
tyrant, 26–28, 33n19, 34n26, 34n27
tyrant's: grasp, 27, 28; head, 27; name, 27

Utopia. *See* Thomas More

Vives, 9, 23

Wells, Robin Headlam, 2, 3n1, 3n6, 22
Wiggins, Martin, 31, 34n32
Witches, 6, 8, 13, 20, 22, 26, 28

www.ingramcontent.com/pod-product-compliance
Lightning Source LLC
Chambersburg PA
CBHW021835300426
44114CB00009BA/453